Praise for *Soul Pain Revealed*

For a fresh look at the cause of mental illness, pick up *Soul Pain Revealed: Bridging Psychology With Faith as the Way Through Suffering*, a well-written, interesting reading experience. Many people think psychological problems are simply due to chemical imbalances and bad upbringings, while others think psychiatric problems are just demonic, which is not accurate. Neither extreme is the true picture, in most cases. Dr. Julie describes a variety of ways to understand mental health problems correctly. More importantly, she addresses the spiritual aspect of emotional distress and suggests new ways that may bring healing more quickly. If you are struggling with your own emotional issues and want a more comprehensive view of what might be the underlying problem, this book is well worth your time.

Dr. Rodney Hogue
Pastor, Author, and Founder of Rodney Hogue Ministries

With this book, Dr. Julie Caton shares a lifetime of experience and insight as a Christian psychologist. By looking at a number of revealing cases, she shows how spiritually informed approaches have helped a number of clients to find healing from very painful pasts, including her own. The book is of particular interest to those looking at counseling approaches in a charismatic or Pentecostal framework.

Joshua Brown, Ph.D.
Professor of Psychological and Brain Sciences

Soul Pain Revealed highlights the importance of having faith in our lives, particularly as a healing agent. Dr. Caton has created an interesting, thorough, but also exciting reading experience. She unpacks the value of faith, which has been so much at the heart of my research. I highly recommend this book to both lay readers and those in the academic world. It certainly boosted my faith.

Harold G. Koenig, M.D.
Professor of Psychiatry and Behavioral Sciences
Duke University Medical Center, Durham, North Carolina

Dr. Julie Caton has made a significant contribution to our understanding of how the human soul reacts to all of the traumatic events that occur in one's life. Her writings bring clarity to the truth of how the soul can be restored and healed from such pain, helping us to live free. As a key to finding release and freedom to the wounds of the soul, I wholeheartedly endorse *Soul Pain Revealed*.

Dr. Mike Hutchings
Director of Education, Global Awakening
Mechanicsburg, Pennsylvania
President, God Heals PTSD Foundation

Christians should not avoid the topic of mental illness, as Dr. Julie Caton helps us realize in her book, *Soul Pain Revealed*. Here she takes a face-to-face look at mental health issues, directly and professionally, and reveals how the power of the Holy Spirit can work in one's emotional life. God desires to heal, using both medicine and His supernatural power. This book looks at the diverse ways in which He brings healing to the mind, will, and emotions.

Dr. Caton combines her professional expertise, personal life experience, and faith in an all-powerful, miracle-working God to create a dynamic treasure trove. This book is clearly born out of Julie's love for God and people, and will bring you further into Kingdom freedom.

Reverend Jack Hempfling
Pastor of Living Waters Church, LeRoy, New York

In *Soul Pain Revealed*, Julie courageously opens her own soul journey for the reader to walk alongside her questions, trials, and victories. With stark knowledge and experience in both worlds, she tackles the conflict that can exist between professional counselors and the Church's healing ministry. It is easy to "hear" her compassion and her desire to bring forth truth and clarity on behalf of the person experiencing soul pain. This is a very clear and necessary document for the professional counselor and healing minister alike. The case studies add credence and readability to the book, which one can read quickly or study deeply to glean the truths held within.

Julie proposes a "new paradigm" in which she suggests a way forward, taking in account all of her personal and professional experience. I can't wait for the follow-up as practitioners of this potent paradigm begin to put its principles into practice!

Leonard C. Hays, Jr., MA, Clinical Psychology
Fatherheart Ministries
Living Loved Project

Dr. Julie Caton's book is an excellent resource to bridge the medical community and divine healing. It focuses on bringing healing to the whole person, especially within the area of mental health. This book is full of testimonies of divine healing and deliverance when one prays in the name of Jesus. We highly recommend it.

William and Chantal Wood
Global Awakening Ministry Team

I am grateful for Dr. Julie Caton's book, *Soul Pain Revealed.* Both psychology and Christian beliefs have truths to bring to the table in working with those who struggle with emotional pain. Facing this task, Dr. Caton brings together knowledge and experience as a Christian psychologist. I particularly value her section on deliverance. Therapists need a working knowledge of deliverance as they facilitate emotional healing with those in pain.

Suzanne Allen, Ph.D., D.Min.
Boston, MA

SOUL PAIN
REVEALED

BRIDGING PSYCHOLOGY
WITH FAITH AS THE WAY
THROUGH SUFFERING

To Patty —
May the LORD
bless you and your
family! So great
meeting You,
Julie Caton

Dr. Julie Caton

 **GROUND TRUTH PRESS**

NASHUA, NEW HAMPSHIRE

Editor: Bonnie Lyn Smith
Cover design: Laura Dudek
Photographer: Laura Dudek
Cover Photograph: Upper Falls, Letchworth State Park, New York

First printing 2019

Printed in the United States of America

Trade paperback ISBN-13: 978-1-7337677-3-6
Trade paperback ISBN-10: 1733767738

Publisher's Cataloging-In-Publication Data
(Prepared by The Donohue Group, Inc.)

Names: Caton, Julie, author.
Title: Soul pain revealed : bridging psychology with faith as the way
    through suffering / Julie Caton, Ph.D.
Description: Nashua, New Hampshire : Ground Truth Press, [2019] |
    Includes bibliographical references and index.
Identifiers: ISBN 9781733767736 (trade paperback) | ISBN 1733767738
    (trade paperback)
Subjects: LCSH: Psychology and religion. | Spiritual healing. | Mental
    illness--Religious aspects--Christianity. | Suffering--Psychological
    aspects. | Suffering--Religious aspects--Christianity.
Classification: LCC BF51 .C38 2019 | DDC 261.515--dc23

2019941526

ACKNOWLEDGMENTS

Thank you very much to the many people who made this book possible. I'm especially grateful to Dr. Randy Clark for his enthusiasm from the beginning and to many of Global Awakening's associates who spoke encouraging words to me. These include, but are not limited to, Suzy and Steve Allen, Blaine Cook, Laurie Gross, Rodney Hogue, Mike Hutchings, Remy Lehner, and William and Chantal Wood. Also, I offer a big thank-you to my fellow students in the Global Awakening Christian Healing Certification Program.

To the people who offered their testimonies—you are the best! Without your transparency, this book would not have been written. To my own grown children, thank you for encouraging me to be transparent as well. Now, others can see how a loving God has redeemed a wounded soul.

I extend my gratitude to the preliminary readers and others who helped in various ways or sent in endorsements: Amy Bolton, Josh Brown, Chauncey Crandall IV, Joshua Dudek, Sue Green, Leonard Hays, Jack Hempfling, Leeland Jones, Heather Kimbriel, Harold Koenig, Randy LeBaron, Craig Miller, Doug Mitchell, Doreen Morehouse, Phill Ohlson, Sherry Snell, and David VanderLinden.

To my prayer warriors of all sorts: Thank you for persevering in prayer for this project and not tiring of hearing me say, "Please pray for the book." Without your support, the obstacles would not have been removed. Your prayers have called forth the Holy Spirit to flow, helping me at times to change course and ultimately to cross the finish line.

A special thank you to Laura Dudek, who has walked alongside me, not only during the creation of this book, but through the development of my other publications and Facebook Bread Basket videos. The Lord has used her to call out the gold in me. The regular support of Jessica Barone and Jacqualine

Chamberlain has eased me through the numerous daily hiccups that have come my way. Finally, I'm indebted to my editor, Bonnie Lyn Smith, who quickly saw the value of this book and has polished it until it shines!

Everyone: For blessing me, may the Lord favor each of you in a special way.

DEDICATION

*I dedicate this book to
The Divine Encourager,
the Truth-Giving Spirit
who expresses God's heart
and delights in revealing mysteries to us.
Thank you, Pneuma.
I love You.*

FOREWORD

by Randy Clark, D. Min.,
Overseer of the Apostolic Network of Global Awakening,
Founder of Global Awakening,
Mechanicsburg, Pennsylvania

During our December 2016 ministry trip to Brazil, Dr. Julie Caton and I shared several hours discussing this much-needed book: *Soul Pain Revealed: Bridging Psychology With Faith as the Way Through Suffering*. It undertakes an assignment dear to my heart because Julie has drawn the elements of mental health treatment together with supernatural principles. We both want answers to this all-encompassing question: How can concerned counselors, who are helping people with mental illness, become more effective?

This book is a must-read for a variety of people: those who are already in the healing professions; those who are expanding their "tools" to be effective counselors on prayer teams; and those who struggle themselves with mental illness. This will open up new options.

Julie and I had met for the first time at Global Awakening's Cultivate Revival in 2015, when she experienced her own miracle healing because of a word of knowledge the Lord had given me. A year later in Brazil, with a team of one hundred trained volunteers, Julie and I saw more than 3,000 healings, some quite miraculous. I remember Julie bounding up to me after she had seen a young woman, paralyzed from birth, walk free of her wheelchair for the first time in her life. Julie's excitement was palpable. Her passion for seeing the healing of this young woman blessed me. Clearly, Julie has a heart for those who are wounded and hurting.

Because of my own history of needing **inner healing** and my commitment in serving those with emotional difficulties, Julie's topic interested me. Years ago while I was in Toronto, I struggled with a strong sense of rejection, from which I was healed. Since then, I have seen the overlap between mental illness and the activity of the **demonic** realm. What most people view as psychological problems today may well stem from dark spiritual activity. The world around us is becoming increasingly complex; we are prone to confusion, delusions, and heartache. **Suicide** is the number two killer of adolescents, second only to car accidents. For these reasons alone, *Soul Pain Revealed: Bridging Psychology With Faith as the Way Through Suffering* is long overdue.

This book offers three contributions: important information within the mental health field, examples of faith experiences to use in counseling, and a description of "tools" beneficial to both of these groups. But she doesn't stop there. She tackles this foundational question: What is the primary ingredient in emotional suffering—and what can we do about it?

While this is not a "self-help" book, it is written in a concise, nonacademic style, so lay readers will benefit from the contents. As Julie summarizes information about medication, defense mechanisms, and therapeutic interventions, she places testimonies throughout, making the factual learning both practical and relevant. These testimonies attest to the power of God as He has activated their victories over mental illness. I love that element of this book because testimonies enhance our faith.

One of my pleasures in reading *Soul Pain Revealed: Bridging Psychology With Faith as the Way Through Suffering* was Julie's life story. With courageous transparency, she shares her own difficulties with depression as she lived through an emotionally abusive marriage. This is a story of personal transformation, of a woman growing in understanding the Holy Spirit's power and facing victories and defeats. She has been a

Christian psychologist for 50 years. Yet, her life has not been easy.

When you finish reading, you will be challenged to consider what this seasoned psychologist has written: Fundamental changes must take place to help people with emotional issues. Julie does not shy away from the basic beliefs Jesus taught: that man's nature is sinful, that emotional health correlates to forgiving one's enemy, and that soul pain can be healed by becoming dependent on God. She believes evil activity and demonic spirits may be the root cause of some of our emotional suffering. I respect her courage for saying that, especially as she wrestles with the difficult question of "What is suffering?" She suggests that Jesus is the antidote to our suffering.

God has called me to be a bridge builder. So I'm pleased this book provides a framework for building bridges between secular psychology and faith-based healing. Julie dives deeply into inner healing and highlights the truth that our "salvation" is a thorough body-soul-spirit recovery. Reading this will kindle a spark for those either needing inner healing and/or for those serving wounded souls. My prayer is that God will use this book to ignite Holy Spirit fire to bring complete soul restoration and emotional freedom to people who suffer.

I am so excited about what I feel are three new books on healing. They reveal the emotional and physical connections we need to understand and share valuable tools for working with those who suffer. These three books are *Soul Pain Revealed: Bridging Psychology With Faith as the Way Through Suffering* by Julie Caton, Ph.D; *Breaking Emotional Barriers to Healing* by Craig A. Miller MS, LMSW, ACSW; and a forthcoming book, *Healing PTSD*, by Mike Hutchings, D.Min., M.Div., who was also a licensed behavioral therapist in Illinois.

CONTENTS

FIGURES

TESTIMONIES

PSYCH 101S

POETRY

INTRODUCTION

There has got to be more—more to helping people with emotional pain and suffering—than meets the eye. This thought has been a driving force throughout my 70 years. When I was a toddler (1950), my parents offset their anxieties by practicing air-raid drills in our basement's "nuclear bomb shelter." As a high school student (1962), I was upset by the injustices of racism embedded in the desegregation movement. By the time I was in college (1966), essays on the dehumanizing influence of slavery on the human personality were required reading and became the topic of my undergraduate thesis.

Clearly, human beings experience deep suffering of a variety of kinds. And try as I might, I did not see long-lasting solutions to these painful problems. When I was a school-age child, I played "family" with two favorite stuffed dolls, solving their problems as I moved them around their cardboard dollhouse. Perhaps this was my first foray into the field of psychology. Once I was in high school, I created an interfaith club where 60 students gathered monthly to hear about the gods of different religions. In September 1963, I thought religion was the solution to man's[1] emotional pain. But, two months later, when the assassination of President John F. Kennedy threw my school, my community, and my country into a tailspin on that November day, I concluded that "faith in god" was not proving to be helpful. I chucked institutional religion out the door.

So, as I entered college and the United States entered the Vietnam War, drafting my classmates and putting their lives on

---

1 Any reference to "man" or "mankind" throughout this document is a reference to all of humankind, both male and female.

the line, I became aware of two important factors: First, I and my fellow human beings faced emotional problems—a condition I call "soul pain," the fate of all humanity. To me, soul pain is the dull ache, hellish darkness, or swirl of anxiety that leaves one wondering what life is really all about. It raises the question: How can I cope with my emotional suffering? The second factor was this: I had come into a personal relationship with Jesus and wondered, "Might there be a solution to soul pain by connecting with Jesus?"

So I set about pursuing these two questions: What is the root cause of my soul pain, and could God offer a psychology of suffering that would heal that pain? This book is a reflection of my journey to discover answers.

I begin with two premises:

1. There is a personal, loving God who wants to be active in our lives.
2. The scientific field of mental health and psychology has developed tools to help alleviate soul pain.

After seven decades doing this search, I have concluded that soul pain can best be relieved only when faith-based resources partner well with science. However, these two landscapes—science and rational thought on one hand, and faith and supernatural beliefs on the other hand—have not been bridged well. Because of the age-old suspicion between rational thinking, which demands scientific evidence, and faith-based beliefs, which rely on supernatural power, there is an existential divide between the two.

When I was 17 years old, I discovered that a faith-based approach to living was important. This has remained so in my life. At the same time, I chose a career in psychology because the principles and skills taught in mental health and psychology programs appeared to be the most immediate way of alleviating soul pain. Hence, I pursued an education in the "sciences" while at the same time living "by faith" for Jesus. However, straddling these two landscapes caused me some problems.

While I faced persecution by the mental health group (i.e., mostly academics who were rational-humanists) and was also criticized by the faith-based group (i.e., people who were skeptical about science and psychological precepts), I discovered a current area of research under way, which was examining the "science of faith." Specifically, academics were studying the benefits of faith on the healing process. Their conclusions stated categorically that a person suffering with ill health showed better improvement when he or she believed in God than one who shunned faith. Furthermore, the researchers proposed that the human brain is wired to believe in God, suggesting that man's well-being may be connected to faith. These findings heralded the potential for the mental health worldview to partner successfully with the faith-based worldview.

The finding that *faith benefits healing* is one of the underlying premises for this book. I have explored soul pain, looking at what the human soul is all about, the cause of its suffering, and how faith in God provides a psychology of well-being. Based on the biblical description of a human being, a person's **soul** is one of three parts in his or her make-up. The other two parts are the body and the spirit. The body is the outer core that houses the soul and spirit. Finally, the spirit is the third aspect of a person; it is responsive to the divine spark of God. The interaction of these three—body, soul, and spirit—is the foundation for psychological health or illness.

The soul, which is comprised of one's thoughts, feelings, and choices, can easily be damaged. Traditionally, resources in the mental health field have been helpful in building sound thinking, stable emotions, and responsible choices. One can see that professionals in the field of mental health have a lot to offer the wounded soul. "Because over three-quarters of psychiatric inpatients have religious needs, it is no longer tenable to ignore the role that religion plays in treating mental illness," according to Dr. Harold Koenig of Duke University.[2]

The tools and remedies suggested by the mental health field can fine-tune solutions to help the soul. Psychological interventions certainly can correct the damage done to one's thoughts, emotions, and conscience through the wear and tear of life.

This book takes a look at how psychological practice and spiritual principles benefit the hurting soul. When one is connected to his or her Creator in a loving, dependent relationship, the person's soul wounds heal. Through this connection, he or she is restored to sound mental health. Yet, mental health interventions do not always succeed in stopping the suffering, as anyone with soul pain can tell you.

After I discuss the human soul, I push deeper and look at the spirit part of a person. I wish my readers to fully understand that mental illness is caused—at the root—by humanity's disconnection from God. I am not saying that someone with mental illness has *chosen* to be disconnected from God. Far from it. Those who are struggling with their emotions desire God's peace more than most people. I am simply highlighting the idea that all human beings live on a "fallen planet," one that has been corrupted over millennia by godlessness. Because of this, many variables negatively influence our bodies, souls, and spirits. Disease factors, DNA anomalies, communication breakdowns, and personality dysfunction are just a few areas of brokenness that enter a person's life and impact mental illness.

On the opposite side of this discussion is the biblical concept that the presence of the power of God in one's life can change these negative influences. To balance this picture, one needs to learn about Christian doctrine, for this is as important as awareness of psychological practices. When people come to

---

2 Harold G. Koenig, M.D., *Faith and Mental Health: Religious Resources for Healing* (Philadelphia: Templeton Foundation Press, 2005), 145.

believe that God indeed plays a role in emotional well-being, they then need to understand the doctrines of Jesus, namely, how spiritual disconnection came about, and how Jesus overcomes it.

Two types of people are the players in this adventure: the "givers" and the "seekers." The first group, the givers, are the counselors, pastors, social workers, psychologists, even the listening "friends"—all who share a desire to *give* support and wisdom for the purpose of relieving soul pain. The second group, the seekers, includes the clients, patients, church members, even the conflicted "friend"; in short, it refers to anyone who comes *seeking* help to relieve his or her pain and gain understanding.

Whether people are givers or seekers, they hold their own unique worldview, which places them somewhere on this continuum of science and faith. On the far end are **rationalism** and **humanism**. Here, we have people who have excluded God from the equation and who believe that the science-minded human being and his secular approaches have the answers. On the other end, we find the faith-filled person who focuses entirely on the supernatural and God as the sole source of healing. As you can guess, the best way to address soul pain is to build a trusting partnership between people in both the field of mental health and the faith-based community (see Figure 1 on page 8). One purpose of this book is to describe this continuum, so that readers can make informed decisions about where they would like to position themselves and why.

The book's conclusion looks at the nature of suffering, a universal human phenomenon produced by soul pain. The emotion of fear is the foundation of this suffering. As I hope you will discover, fear is an outcome of man's choice to be independent from God, instead of being dependent on God. Because the Creator desires His people to experience well-being and to be free of soul pain, God provides a solution in the Person of Jesus.

I believe there is an **enemy of our souls** (Satan, aka the devil, Lucifer). Soul pain is not simply the result of damage to our thoughts, feelings, and conscience, resulting from biological, psychological, and social factors. The human soul can be injured by dark forces. The enemy attacks people through ungodly beliefs, generational curses, and other demonic influences originating in the supernatural. One of the enemy's primary weapons is instilling us with the fear of our death. Fortunately, Jesus is the victor over this fear because Jesus promises resurrection, freedom from the threat of death, and a life with God for eternity. The doctrine of Jesus as Savior stomps on that fear, dissolving it entirely and pulling the rug completely out from under the enemy and his stranglehold on us.

I have woven my journey's story of these discoveries throughout the book. At certain points, an academic topic is highlighted and clarified, so I have labeled it "Psych 101."

A glossary list for mental health terms appears in Appendix A. A glossary of faith-based terms within Christian subculture is also included (Appendix B). It could be helpful to the non-Christian to read through this list before reading the entirety of this book to gain a better understanding of Christian culture. Words that appear in that list are bolded in the text. Footnotes can be used to build a bibliography for the various areas of interest.

I include vignettes about people I've met, changing their names, in order to illustrate certain points. There are 12 testimonies written by different individuals. Some of them have requested that their names be changed; others were comfortable identifying themselves. Their testimonies are placed within the contents where appropriate.

My life calling has been to bring words of life and health to people. But, sadly, I have not always been successful doing that for myself. This book describes a 50-year journey of overcoming depression, healing heart wounds, and finding repair for my own soul.

With some trepidation, I have chosen to be transparent. I weave my personal saga throughout so that you can participate with me in this process of discovery. I pray you will benefit from stepping into my life and observing how God has helped me.

During the times I struggled with my own emotional difficulties and life challenges, I was learning the informational content incorporated in this book. Hopefully, you can observe how academic head knowledge has been transformed into heart knowledge, thus resulting in successful healing.

Day by day, year by year, God instilled these truths into me at work and at home. The full tuition I paid to learn about the psychology of suffering was the soul pain acquired along my own journey. I give thanks to God that I have walked through the dark tunnel and have come out with a restored soul.

This is my heart for all people: to gain emotional health by successfully managing the suffering and trials of life. My desire for your life is the same as God's desire—that you will experience complete well-being and also that you will help others find restoration for their souls along the way.

Figure 1

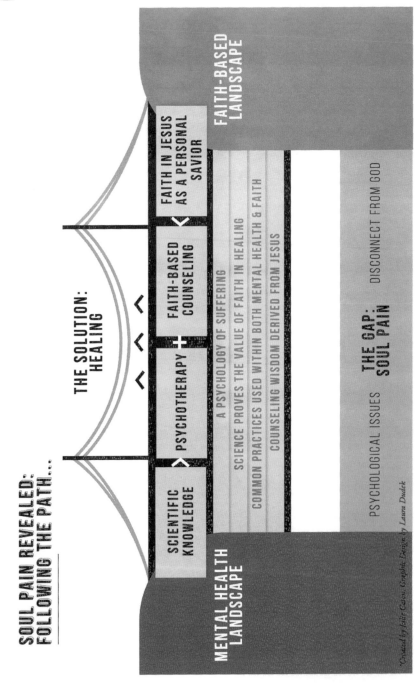

Broken
by Julie Caton

While mowing,
  A stone explodes into a glass pane,
    Shattering the window—Broken.

While cooking,
  The egg slips onto the tile floor,
    Splattering yolk and shell—Broken.

While working,
  The laptop tips off the desk,
    Cracking its back, losing its data—Broken.

While relaxing,
  My reunion mug slides from my grasp,
    Hitting the floor, smashing into pieces—Broken.

While crying,
  My painful wrist flails corkscrewed,
    Fractured by a tumble off a horse—Broken.

While married,
  My heart is severed into pulsing tissue
    By my friend's hostility and anger—Broken.

While taking communion,
  A fresh loaf of bread to be eaten by believers
    Is ripped apart—Broken.

While worshipping,
  The Carpenter Messiah, forsaken and dying,
    Is crucified anew—Broken.

While believing,
  The stone is rolled away,
    Sundering the seal on Jesus's empty tomb—Broken.

While submitting,
  Selfishness and pride crush my soul;
    I am yielding—Broken.

AND THEN REDEEMED!

PART ONE:

EXPLORING THE LANDSCAPE OF MENTAL HEALTH

1
WHY SOUL PAIN IS ALIVE
AND WELL ON PLANET EARTH

The Search Begins

PEOPLE ASK ME: "How long have you been a psychologist?"
Or: "How many years have you been providing counseling?"
As far back as I can remember, my heart's desire was to help
hurting people, to fix their problems, and to offer advice. In the
introduction, I mentioned that as a child I spent hours with my
two dolls, resolving their arguments while I moved them through
cardboard rooms. I felt not only their pain but also mine and that
of others as well, and I wanted to soothe us all.

I must have been born with a drive to make others happy,
with a God-given compassion for heartbroken people in this
unjust world. Most of my childhood was focused on finding
peace and discovering how to manage suffering. I realized my
ability to ease people's problems and relieved my own pain in the
process. Curious to the nth degree, I delved into ideas, read
incessantly, and challenged people to give me answers.

Soul pain can have its roots in one's culture. My growing-
up years followed the horrors of the concentration camps by only
a decade, and the Cold War raged on. Also, this was the tense era
of desegregation. Our black and white televisions showed the
National Guard protecting the black children as they walked
bravely into white classrooms.

Today's culture finds children facing the threat of terrorism,
human trafficking, and school violence. Because of social media,

our children have access to all sorts of psychologically unhealthy stimuli and are vulnerable to cyber bullying. Added to these variables, this upcoming generation seems to be parented by Google. Whatever children seek out on YouTube is building their capacity for relating to others (or not). All these factors influence the emotional sickness we see around us.

I am grateful for my fairly healthy, early home environment (1946-1966) in southern Connecticut. Dad commuted to New York City to work in financial research. Mom, a country club wife and a Junior League volunteer, took charge of our lives and provided the physical basics for my older brother, my younger sister, and me. Sadly, my mother carried a lot of anger and anxiety; her critical nature put a lifelong strain on our relationship and left me struggling with feelings of rejection into my adulthood. Our family was argumentative and unaffectionate. While my parents encouraged attendance at a Presbyterian church, their spirits were not ignited by God during the time I was growing up. However, I participated in the children's choir, where I found that singing wonderful words about God whetted my spiritual appetite.

Circumstances wounded me deeply when I was in fifth grade. Classmates flung bad names at me, shunned me, and excluded me in sports and parties. While I watched my former friends chat on the opposite side of the street, my heart would break because no one talked to me. My sense of self was shattering. If I had trusted others before that time, my trust capacity plummeted that year. I was a sad, confused 10-year-old who had no clue how to make life work.

During high school, I stabilized socially but was hungry spiritually, so I created a club called "The Interfaith Club." At the high school, about 60 students attended our monthly meetings. We explored Hinduism, Judaism, Baha'i World Faith, Christian Science—you name it, we probably discussed it.

On November 22, 1963, I was driving from school to the local railroad station to pick up that month's club presenter. He was an Orthodox Jewish rabbi, commuting an hour from New York City to teach us about the Hebrew God.

At 2:10 p.m., my car radio music crackled and the announcer broke through: "We interrupt this program to announce that the President of the United States, John F. Kennedy, has been assassinated in Dallas." Shocked, but knowing I had to get the rabbi, I kept driving and listening. When I arrived at the station, the rabbi was easy to spot with his long black coat with tails, a chest-length beard, and a rigid black hat. His long curls bounced under his ears. The rabbi and I had never met; we had only talked on the phone to plan that afternoon's meeting. I said my name by way of introduction and reached out my hand to shake his. Swallowing back my stifled tears, I said, "You probably don't know this yet, but our president has just been assassinated."

The rabbi blanched and gasped. Then he let out a sob and unabashedly wept. He continued crying as I drove him back to the school to figure out what we should do.

School was in chaos. The loudspeaker provided updates. Teens and teachers alike were crying. Parents rushed to pick up their children as though the world were ending. Tears ran down the face of our faculty sponsor, an older, dignified woman whom I had looked up to in the past year. She could barely catch her breath. Her demonstration of this level of pain scared me.

The club meeting was cancelled. Later, I arrived home to find my shocked parents pouring their cocktails earlier than usual to calm their nerves. During that never-to-forget weekend, my parents, 14-year-old sister, and I camped in front of the television watching the world view the death of our president over and over again on the "tube." Everything was unraveling.

At that the moment in my life, I chucked institutionalized religion. With all I was observing, including the horror of our president being shot and killed, I concluded that religion was not providing real answers. The people around me, who were "followers," obviously weren't finding solace in their respective

15

belief systems. My parents' faith, such as it was, offered me nothing. Where was a benevolent God in all of this chaos?

In that needy season, I met a staff woman from an evangelical organization; she encouraged me to read the recorded history of Jesus of Nazareth. She said, "Don't read the Gospels based on what you learned in Sunday school. Don't assess who this man is from the point of view of your mother's prayer book. Read about Jesus with fresh eyes. Look at what He did, what He said, and how He handled life. See what you think of Him for yourself." This may have been one of the best pieces of advice I've ever received.

During a youth rally of 500 teenagers on April 17, 1964, my life was changed forever. I heard a powerful message about Jesus's crucifixion. Overwhelmed, I escaped to our Atlantic City hotel room, laid on my bed in broad daylight, stuffed my head into my pillow, and cried, "Jesus, I am making a mess of living. **I commit my life to you.**"

An hour earlier, I had heard the purpose of Jesus's crucifixion for the first time in my life. God gave me a love message: "Julie, even though you are messing up your life, Jesus willingly laid down His life on the cross for you. We can fix yours. My Son allowed the soldiers to nail His hands and feet to the wood, get hoisted up, and then die. He did this just for you."

The truth that Jesus loved me penetrated my heart. Even though I was selfish, angry, and unforgiving, He took my confusions, hurts, and all of me that was broken, onto Himself. He did this simply because He loved me.

I did not have all the "spiritual" vocabulary I have now. So that day, when feelings of freedom and loving warmth washed over me, I didn't know it was the **Holy Spirit** entering me. I didn't realize God had given me a divine gift in the Comforter and Helper who was already changing my life. I had been "**born again.**"

When I arrived home, my mother was sick in bed. This was a unique happening, as my mother was one of those tough nuts that never succumbed to weakness. But, while I was gone, she had been diagnosed with pleurisy and ordered to bed for a week. Without my giving it a thought, God's love kicked in.

"Mom, is there anything I can do to help?" I asked. Keep in mind that this offer was coming from a typically self-centered 17-year-old who rarely offered to do anything for her family. My temper fizzled away and my heart melted with God's love. He had changed me.

The **conversion experience** set me on the right road, but it did not answer all my questions. My life still felt uncertain. The world around me seemed threatening. What was the source of my soul pain and psychological confusion? What was I missing? What was I failing to understand?

One day when I was in biology class, the science teacher was explaining the life of organisms. She said, "Even human beings are nothing but a process of oxidation and combustion." A brash boy jumped out of his seat. His face turned red, and he defiantly threw out this question to the class: "Is that right? Really? Then what kind of meaning does life have?" My heart echoed his.

Fifty years later, working as a therapist, I still hear these cries for answers:

- "What is the purpose of existence?"
- "Is there a God?"
- "Why am I alive?"
- "Why do bad things happen to good people?"

These types of questions plagued me in my college years, which was a season in which African Americans struggled to find their voice during the desegregation movement. I wrote my Bachelor's degree thesis on the characteristics of the Negro Slave

Personality.[3] In the midst of this project, I discovered some answers to my big questions about humanity.

During the same season, at the same time, Jewish Americans, whose parents were survivors of the concentration camps, were speaking out about the holocaust, and *The Diary of Anne Frank* was mandatory reading in English classes. Viktor Frankl, a concentration camp survivor and psychiatrist, wrote: "The spiritual dimension in man cannot be ignored because it is what makes us human."[4]

I pondered these questions, read Viktor Frankl and other philosophers, and studied the testimonies of African-American slave grandparents and holocaust survivors. One common theme emerged: We human beings have souls. Whether one is a Negro slave, a concentration camp prisoner, or a kid being bullied, we have this part of our humanity called "the soul." Today, I believe the soul is that which makes us human. The soul hungers to discover how to survive and to manage life's stresses.

For more than 50 years I have thought about this question:

What is my soul?

The mystery of mental illness is discovered only when we understand the human soul.

The Root of Mental Illness Nests in One's Soul

As a new follower of Jesus, I studied the Bible to find answers. **The birth of the human soul is described in the Creation narrative.** When God created man, He formed Adam out of the ground's dust and breathed into him the breath of life.[5]

---

3 Julie Vanderbilt Brown, *The Nature of Negro Slave Personality: An Analysis* (Honors Thesis for Smith College American Studies, February 1968).

4 Viktor E. Frankl, *The Doctor and the Soul: From Psychotherapy to Logotherapy* (New York: Alfred A. Knopf, 1955), ix.

5 Genesis 2:7

That breath of God made man a living creature, a model of Himself. Just as God is one living deity in three parts (Father, Son, and Holy Spirit), the Almighty God made Adam in three parts: **a body, soul, and spirit.**[6] God's intention was to create a perfect human being, complete with a healthy body, a thriving soul, and a responsive spirit.

God wanted man to be in a love relationship with Him, but He could not force love. So God gave us free choice. Enfolded in that opportunity of choice, we were given the freedom to obey God or not. Sadly, Adam and Eve succumbed to Satan's temptation and **chose disobedience**. The devil tempted the first human beings with words that sounded remarkably like this: "Oh folks, are you sure you want to do things God's way? It might be better for you if you took control of your own lives. Why don't you do things the way you want?" And the first man and woman said, "Ok! Sounds good. We'll do things our way."

From that point forward, our forefathers decided to take things into their own hands. The consequence of their disobedience to God was their being disconnected from the Spirit of God. This action caused them physical, emotional, and spiritual pain. **The life, death, and resurrection of Jesus is God's plan to <u>redeem</u> man from that pain. Being redeemed results in being reconnected with the Spirit of God.**

The cause of mankind's dysfunction and the root of humanity's suffering is this disconnection from one's original spiritual source. This separation of the human soul from the Spirit of God is at the heart of mental illness.

Let's look at the structure of a human being more closely. Why body, soul, and spirit? At birth, the human soul indwells a physical body. The baby's soul has the potential for God's Spirit hovering within. But these **three parts of body-soul-spirit are undeveloped.** The body, in its infant stage, continues to grow from the once-fertilized egg into physical maturity. The soul, with

---

6 1 Thessalonians 5:23

its thoughts, feelings, and will, also matures. However, the human being's spirit is dormant, waiting to be awakened by the Spirit of God.

Scripture tells us that the Lord, who "stretches out the heavens, who lays the foundation of the earth…forms the human spirit within a person."[7] Because the human being's ultimate purpose is to become both fully human and spiritually regenerated, at the beginning of a baby's existence, his soul starts the process of connecting with the Spirit of God. As one's physical body grows, so does his soul. We see this in the child's increased ability to think in the abstract. Also, his capacity to identify and regulate his emotions takes shape, and his conscience (his will or the part of him that makes a choice) is formed. During the time when his soul is maturing, the human being is also making decisions (or not) about yoking his spirit with the Spirit of God. So, in his process of maturing, one's soul is being influenced directly by both the human spirit and the Holy Spirit. Hopefully, the end result of his development is his being **born again in the image of God**.

My belief is that the human's **tripartite soul holds the key to mental illness** (see Figure 2 on page 22). A separation of the soul from God can cause the emotional problems facing us today.[8] When one's soul is in sync with one's body and is aligned with the Spirit of the Creator, it is healthy. That means one's physical behavior, thoughts, feelings, and choices are being divinely managed. Conversely, an unhealthy soul is out of alignment with God and is not plugged into God's power source. Eventually, the stress of life wears the body and the soul down. Some physical and/or emotional illness results from the body storing emotional trauma in its cells or from repressed psychological pain. [See *Psych 101: Medication and Brain Anatomy*.]

---

7 Zechariah 12:1

8 Leonard Sweet and Frank Viola, *Jesus: A Theography* (Nashville: Thomas Nelson, 2012), 41.

Given the idea that a healthy soul is the basis for sound mental health, we face this question: **How does a soul acquire good psychological health**? Perhaps it's easier to look at the other side of the coin—that of mental illness. What kinds of choices does a soul make about dealing with stress, that might cause mental illness? What does he do to avoid or decrease his pain? To fully understand mental illness, we need to look at the factors involved with emotional disturbance.

Figure 2

BODY-SOUL-SPIRIT CONNECTION

	OUTCOME	MAN'S WAY	**KEYS TO GOD'S WAY: FAITH + GRACE** OR	GOD'S WAY	OUTCOME
SPIRIT	DEATH *For the wages of sin is death.* Romans 6:23	OWN SPIRIT RELIES ON SELF *The Lord detests all the proud of heart... They will not go unpunished.* Proverbs 16:5		HOLY SPIRIT *"Repent and be baptized, every one of you, in the name of Jesus Christ for the forgiveness of your sins. And you will receive the gift of the Holy Spirit."* Acts 2:38	LIFE *For it is by grace you have been saved through faith... the gift of God.* Ephesians 2:8
SOUL	BONDAGE *We... were enslaved under the basic forces of the world.* Galatians 4:3 NET	MIND *For what I want to do, I do not do, but what I hate I do.* Romans 7:15 EMOTIONS *The heart is deceitful above all things and beyond cure.* Jeremiah 17:9 WILL/CHOOSER *For they ... chose not to fear the LORD... therefore, they must eat the bitter fruit of living their own way.* Proverbs 1:29 NLT		MIND OF CHRIST *We have the mind of Christ.* 1 Corinthians 2:16 FRUIT OF THE SPIRIT *The fruit of the Spirit is love, joy, peace, forbearance...* Galatians 5:22-23 JESUS AS LORD *Christ may dwell in your hearts through faith.* Ephesians 3:17	SPIRITUAL FREEDOM *"You will know the truth, and the truth will set you free... The Son sets you free."* JOHN 8:32, 36
BODY	SICKNESS *As you continue in your rebellion... the whole head is sick. And the whole heart is faint.* Isaiah 1:5, NASB	MAN'S WAY OF LIVING *If ... you refuse to listen... you will not live a long, good life.* Deuteronomy 30:17-18 NLT		GOD'S WAY OF LIVING *Your bodies are the temples of the Holy Spirit.* 1 Corinthians 6:19	HEALED *Enjoy good health.* 3 John 1:2

Created by Julie Caton, Graphic Design by Laura Dudek

2
HOW DO PEOPLE HANDLE SOUL PAIN?

INITIALLY, WHEN PAINFUL emotions and confusing thoughts are experienced by a person, he naturally starts to compensate for them. For example, an infant being disturbed by high levels of anxiety in his environment, may stop eating, become constipated, or cry incessantly. An adult facing excessive stress may turn to addictive behaviors or sink into depression as a way of managing. The following sections focus on these typical responses to soul pain. What are some of the common behavioral changes people experience in order to cope? What are the fundamental questions with which people struggle in their efforts to manage the difficulties of life? Not only do I outline both the traits of mental illness, but also I highlight some characteristics of emotional well-being.

Traits of Mental Illness

If you are a giver, you need to be able to discern traits of mental illness in the person you are helping. If you can't, you may set yourself up for unrealistic expectations. If you are a seeker, you need to become self-aware and admit that you may be struggling with one or more of these behaviors.

When a person's soul experiences discomfort, he can respond in a variety of ways. These coping strategies can be conscious or unconscious plans used by the person to ward off emotional pain. For example, he can drive himself harder into life's activities. Or, he can sit down in the corner, give up, and contemplate taking his own life. Perhaps he might seek relief from an external source, such as taking medication, entering psychotherapy, or talking to some type of physician or pastor.

When I first meet a new client, I will ask the seeker, "Why are you here?" Most of them say: "I want to be happier." Truth be told, I don't think the goal of "gaining happiness" is a good reason for being in therapy. While it is a pleasant outcome, happiness is a result of what happens *to* you. It is derived from the "happenings" in your life. In therapy, the goal should be to help one respond well to whatever is occurring in his life, not necessarily to gain happiness. I suggest an alternative goal to happiness. Let's seek after *joy*. This is both an emotional and a spiritual trait conveying an expectation of gladness and the fulfillment of one's desires.

When I interview new seekers, I prod them about "why" they are in therapy. These comments commonly become their answers:

- "Well, I have problems getting along with others."
- "My spouse tells me I have anger issues."
- "I can't manage at work because I'm anxious most of the time."
- "I feel empty and hopeless."

These concerns reflect varying degrees of poor mental health. The one thing they all have in common, however, is that the seeker's **soul is experiencing pain**.

The following are overviews of the **typical symptoms that bring a person into therapy**. Understanding the distinctions between these emotional problems may help the giver relate to the seeker more effectively. On the flip side, the seeker may have a better understanding of what is at the root of his problems.

Someone struggling with **depression** may feel sad and empty, lacking pleasure in living. She may feel ashamed and guilty, and be so hopeless she wishes to die. She can't concentrate, and her mind loops around in unproductive thinking. Her weight is increasing (from overeating) or decreasing (can't eat). Her sleep is too little or too much. Her energy is depleted. The following apt description of depression was written in 1959 by Raymond Cramer:

> In a depression we are let down too far into a hole of despair. The hole becomes very narrow at the top and we cannot see the light of day. A normal person does not slip down so far— he is able to crawl out on his own.[9]

If you are talking with a seeker and suspect he is experiencing suicidal thinking, do not shy away from asking about that. If you know a person fitting this description who reports a **suicide plan, seek professional help** immediately. Do not chide him about his "negative thinking" and tell him to "buck up." That may make matters worse and deepen his depression.

According to the 2016 statistics published by the American Association of Suicidology,[10] about every 12 minutes, one person commits suicide. For every suicide, another six people are directly affected by the loss of the victim. So based on these rates, 250,000 people per year experience heartbreaking pain as a result of suicide. A startling statistic is this: Just over half of female-to-male transgender adolescents have reported attempting suicide, according to *Pediatrics*.[11]

When people with depression have faith in God and anticipate a heavenly, eternal existence after their death, their worldview often dampens their suicidal impulses. They might feel, "I won't do it because I know it would displease God," or "If I kill myself, I'm not sure I will go to heaven. I want heaven, so I won't." Over the years, working in hospitals and clinics, I have become familiar with people contemplating suicide. I have even performed **mental post-mortems** on cases that ended in suicide, which are meetings in which we look at factors influencing these tragic events. Usually, the victims have reported that they do not believe in a higher power or eternal existence. Their environment

9 Raymond L. Cramer, *The Psychology of Jesus and Mental Health* (Grand Rapids: Zondervan, 1959), 63.

10 Facts & Statistics | American Association of Suicidology, accessed April 8, 2019. http://www.suicidology.org/resources/facts-statistics.

11 Russell B. Toomey et al., "Suicide Risk Greatest in Female-Male Transgender Teens," *Pediatrics* (2018). doi:10.1542/peds.2017-4218.

was often dark, unbelieving, and despairing. Whenever people harbor irrational ideas or hear audible whispers such as "Why don't you end it all?" these thoughts often propel the victims to pull the trigger, hang the noose, or crash the car. While I cannot directly see into the spiritual realm, people have reported to me that demonic presences may have influenced suicide attempts.

Let me share the testimony of Erin, who struggled with depression and suicidal thinking. Recently, she participated in a **deliverance ministry** and received freedom from the strongholds and voices that had been harassing her.

Erin's Testimony: Overcoming the Thought of Suicide

I'm Erin, a mom and wife in her mid-30s. Before I came to know Jesus, I'd been haunted by thoughts of suicide because my father took his own life when I was five years old. I think my father's suicide set me up to attempt to take my own life by overdosing when I was 19. Recently I learned that there has been an ancestral spirit of suicide wounding my extended family for many years.

When my father killed himself, I felt rejected. How else could a five-year-old understand her father's death? Why did he leave me? Wasn't I good enough for him? Those were my questions. His abrupt death left a big hole inside of me.

As I grew older, I started thinking that any type of attention might fill the void. I just wanted to be loved. This deep need caused another problem: It set me up to fall victim to my grandfather and my uncle sexually molesting me. My grandfather didn't give a darn about my feelings. He took what he wanted when he wanted it. His behavior caused me to believe many lies: "I didn't matter!" "I didn't deserve respect!" "I had no voice!" Because of this man, my idea of love was twisted. I saw myself as a dirty little girl. I grew up with that negative spirit of "I'm not worth anything."

By 12 years old, I sought out boys, believing the looks and touches they gave me were the same as love. I lost my virginity at 14, hoping to find—what? Love? Something meaningful about life in their arms? Once I gave them what they wanted, they rejected me and turned to others. Such a stupid game! But I kept on playing it.

Many negative spirits flowed around me during these years. Various voices would speak in my head: "You will always be rejected because you are just a dirty little girl." Or: "People you love will abandon you; you are not good enough for anyone."

My emotional life was scarred in another way. Three key women in my life abandoned their children. Whatever their reasons—whether they dumped their kids for a man or rejected them for their own personal freedom—I don't know. But this is what I saw as I grew into my teen years. And I vowed I would never do that. Somehow I would break that cycle of rejection. Yet I did not have a clue as to how.

Today, I believe there is an enemy of our soul. As I look back, the enemy kept poking at me through the hurts of my father's suicide, the humiliation of my relatives sexually abusing me, and my mother. She had been dealing with her problems by overusing alcohol. I got pregnant four times between the ages of 14 and 19.

At the time of my first pregnancy, my mother drove me to Planned Parenthood, where a worker there deceived me about the moral choice I was making, as well as the physical discomfort and heartache that would follow. She assured me: "Oh, ending your pregnancy is a smart decision. You certainly don't want to ruin your future by—you know," and she would glance at my belly. She never once used the word "baby." As I went through that process, I lost sight of the value of life. Death seemed an ugly but natural choice. I couldn't think of any other option.

When I was 16, I became pregnant again and decided to carry this baby. At full-term, I had a beautiful daughter, and we lived with her father for about a year. I tried getting my high school degree, but that went downhill. After her father left us, to support my daughter and me, I went to work as an exotic dancer.

It was fun for a while. But I slid into drugs, alcohol, more men, and the lure of money and material things. I was still seeking fulfillment in all the wrong places. Most of the time, I felt disappointed in life, rejected by God, and very ashamed when it came to my daughter because of the situations I was putting her through. The hole in my soul just got deeper and darker.

When my daughter was almost three years old, I found myself very depressed. The current man in my life had just broken up with me. So one night I locked myself in the bathroom and took painkillers by the handful in an attempt to kill myself. The voices egged me on: "You have no reason to live." "Just end it."

Then I heard a light knocking at the door. "Mommy, are you ok?" My daughter's voice jolted me back to reality. What saved me was the fact that on the other side of the door was a precious little girl who wanted her Mommy. That was God at work.

I asked her to call her grandma, and before I knew it, I was in the emergency room, with a tube down my throat, having my stomach pumped clean of the lethal overdose. A terrible experience.

My suicide attempt was a result of my being rejected yet again and feeling hopeless. I had no knowledge of a Creator or the love of Jesus. So ending my life was not a difficult decision. The darkness seemed to demand it. Up until that point, I placed no value on my or other peoples' lives.

Several years later, when I was 21, God made another appearance in my life. I met the man who is currently my husband. God sent him to be my angel from heaven. This mature, handsome man had committed himself to God years before and did not partake in the kind of sin in which I was involved. Soon we were attending church together, and a few months later, I had my first actual conversation with a minister about Jesus.

The lady pastor listened well to my story. When she asked about my faith, I told her I would surrender my life to Jesus. She was so encouraging. Then, I shared my current crisis and said: "So you see, I'm pregnant again, and I have to take some blood tests. There is a 75 percent chance I have HIV. I don't know what to do! I've not told my new husband this news."

She comforted me. Then she said something I will never forget: "You now have Jesus, and everything will be ok." Just those simple words settled my heart into believing that everything would work out. I felt a weight lift off my shoulders. My heart filled with God's love.

That born-again experience happened 18 years ago. Since then, I have learned so much by reading the Bible, attending church, and listening to Christian podcasts. This past spring I had a profound experience when I entered into a three-hour ministry with a couple. Their goal was to help me find freedom. I wanted to be set free from any ungodly beliefs or ancestral toxins, as there seemed to be so many in my past.

From this couple, I learned that much of what I had gone through during my childhood, including my own suicide attempt, was influenced by demonic strongholds. To name a few, there had been strongholds of rejection, abandonment, suicide and premature death, not to mention drugs and alcohol. All were under the influence of demonic spirits.

The couple taught me a bondage-breaking prayer, which I use often when any pervasive lies or negative scripts pop into my head. I have felt emotional and spiritual chains break off. Before I met with this deliverance ministry team, I did not know that we could get tangled up in strongholds. I did not believe that demonic spirits could affect one's life. But during the session, the couple helped me to identify several dark spirits, which we cast to the feet of Jesus. I could sense that weight lift off me—literally.

Today, I know my new identity in Jesus. I am someone who is deeply loved by God, beautiful, forgiven, and wonderfully complex. I have been created perfectly by God, and made righteous through Jesus. With this spiritual freedom, partnering with my husband, I am now empowered to lead my children into the next generation free from any darkness. Thank you, Jesus!

Erin, wife, mother, and warrior in the kingdom of God

More Traits of Mental Illness

On the other end of the emotional pole from depression, we find a person miserable (or strangely elated) because he is in a **manic episode**. He is so energized that his speech is rapid, his ideas fly all around, and his behavior is relentless. Usually he has a decreased need for sleep and demonstrates poor judgment. He gets involved with activities that result in painful consequences and pursues unrealistic goals. His **mania** comes in waves, lasting a few hours or even enduring for several months.

A person with an **anxiety disorder** can be as revved up as someone who is manic, but this person reports feeling an inner restlessness most of the time, and she has erratic sleep. She worries incessantly and can't control her thinking. She becomes irritated easily and is forgetful and distractible. She can slide into a **panic attack**, characterized by a rapid heartbeat and difficulty breathing.

Emotions are only one marker of mental health; they do not offer the full picture. A giver must also assess the seeker's **capacity to function** in work, school, and the community.[12] Our emotions are fickle, subject to physical health, hormones, external stress, and even the weather. For this reason, the giver needs to explore one's functioning level. Can the person sustain a stable relationship with others? Can he hold down a job? When people have severe mental illness, they fail at these things. They may

---

12 Again, for the purposes of this book, "giver" represents a counselor, psychiatrist, or faith-based practitioner, even a friend to the person suffering, while "seeker" refers to the patient or person who is suffering and requesting help.

stop doing the basic tasks of living, such as maintaining personal hygiene, exercising self-care, and using socially appropriate speech. Frequently, they self-medicate with drugs and alcohol, making the problems worse.

Another clue to the quality of someone's psychological well-being is the accuracy of a seeker's sense of **reality**. Is he perceiving the world the way most people do, or is he distorting it? This question explores the quality of his thinking and may or may not have anything to do with his feelings. For example, if a person *thinks* everyone is out to get him, in most situations he is wrong and is misperceiving reality, but, because of his paranoid thinking, he genuinely *feels* suspicious and distrustful. His distorted perception of reality needs to be corrected (not his emotions) because poor thinking is the cause of his negative feelings.

Further characteristics of mental stability include the quality of one's *relationships*. Does the seeker behave in safe and empathic ways, and avoid harming other people? Can he adjust and adapt to stress? Can he manage problems in a self-confident and unselfish manner? Repeated patterns of inflexibility, entitlement, and destructive behavior obviously suggest degrees of mental illness. Affirmative answers indicate good mental health.

Ed, a colleague in the mental health field, was eager to share his testimony when he first learned about this project. His story illustrates much of what is discussed here, including manic behavior, paranoid thinking, institutionalization, and problems with daily functioning.

Ed's Testimony:
A Battle Against Schizophrenia

I was crazy—literally—in May 1982. This story is about my falling into a major mental illness and then being given the grace to recover. This testimony has the potential to release healing. Four years earlier, my girlfriend pressured me into asking Jesus into my life. This I did, but halfheartedly. I was afraid my Catholic family would reject me if I made "a decision for Christ." Between 1978 and 1982, through various people, Jesus called me, wooed me, and urged me into His kingdom. But I remained stubborn.

Then one day, after listening to a taped sermon, I finally broke down and repented. It felt like a plug had been pulled and I was flooded with sorrow. So filled with amazement at the love of Jesus, I cried for 10 days and couldn't sleep or eat. My thoughts became extreme. I imagined I was like a John the Baptist and then like Jesus. Perhaps I, too, needed to die on a cross because I was destined to usher in hope for humanity.

When I was baptized with water a week later, I couldn't get out of the baptismal tank, literally. I felt paralyzed. My bizarre behaviors and grandiose thoughts expanded. Really late one night, I went to my mother, weeping and repenting. But this just scared her. Then I told my sister if she continued to raise her kids as Jehovah's Witnesses, she might as well take a gun and shoot them. (She told me a year later that I had said I would shoot them.) My roommate thought something <u>demonic</u> had happened to me and started praying. A loud hissing sound come out of me, like a cloth being ripped out of my gut.

On the tenth day from the onset of this manic behavior, I was admitted to a psychiatric hospital. As we drove there, oppression suffocated me. I was attacked by severe back pain and started screaming that I was dying. My reality was distorted. Once we arrived, I fought the orderlies and wouldn't take medication, believing they were poisoning me.

Once medicated, I slept for 12 hours, my first sleep in days. When I awoke, I wandered into the room of a man. His face morphed into the form of my older brother, and I saw a "synopsis" of a traumatic landscape, which represented our family in earlier years when my brother was horribly abused. I lost it emotionally, and the staff had to escort me back to my room. After several hours in four-point restraints, I settled down. Sadly, the rest of my nine-day stay was marked by continued paranoia and agitation. Every announcement on the hospital's public address system was conspiring to harm me. Every television voice was a threat against me. The staff loaded me up with megadoses of antipsychotic medication. Thankfully, I had a compassionate therapist, who finally sent me home.

Now, I was still crazy, just less so. Through the local mental health center, I was placed on shots of Prolixin, which acted like a horse tranquilizer. After three days at home, intense back pain returned and I felt that same oppression. So I requested a readmission.

This time a different male patient thrust his finger in my face and yelled, "You're the one responsible for Jesus dying on the cross." Tears shot out of my eyes because I believed him. A nurse feared that I was suicidal.

The compassionate therapist encouraged me to get my act together. She said, "You have four days to prove you are safe, or a judge will write a court order forcing a 90-day stay in the state psychiatric hospital." When I said, "I can keep it together," they released me but mandated me to stay on medication and receive outpatient treatment.

That summer of 1983, while I continued therapy at Evergreen Counseling, my medication was changed to Lithium, which was also paralyzing. I slept an average of 12 hours a day, gained 45 pounds, and drooled on myself. I was listless, void of all emotions, and felt dead inside.

My recovery started after I detoxed from all the medication, something the Holy Spirit led me to do. I moved out of my parents' home and back into my own apartment. Healing is a process and takes time. Life began to improve because I was surrounded by supportive friends, a good church, and a strong desire to fulfill my destiny as a believer in Christ.

In June 1984, the Lord brought me to an amazing Christian therapist, Pearl. She spoke life and health into me. I told her, "If I could ever help anyone who suffers like I did from overmedication, I want to do that." She encouraged me to go back to school, and I eventually started working at the same mental health center where I had been a patient. I even worked in an ER, helping to evaluate and often hospitalize mentally ill patients. Honestly, when the orderlies were putting out-of-control people in their restraints, I had to turn away.

This psychotic break in my young adult years was a culmination of crummy things happening as a kid. Also, my brain chemistry went awry, and the enemy actively started working on me because I had stepped into the kingdom of God. My story is about restoration. I am contending for major mental illnesses to be healed. Disconnection from God makes people sick. While the enemy moves in to destroy minds, we pray for restoration with the authority of Jesus; this helps people discover the enemy has no power over them.

In 2006, at a healing conference, I experienced God topping off my own healing by restoring my brain chemistry to full health. In 2012, I asked Randy Clark whether he had ever seen a person with **schizophrenia** healed. He cited a story of a man instantly healed via a pastor in Texas. Randy stated: "Being healed from schizophrenia is akin to a person growing a limb out." He quoted Psalm 103:3, that "God does heal ALL our diseases."

As a licensed social worker, I've worked at our area's primary psychiatric facility and asked myself: "Why shouldn't the people hospitalized here be healed?" Praying for psychotic patients is uncharted territory. But restoration means bringing people back to health. We can use our authority in Christ to pray for the re-creation of a healthy brain, just as we can pray for a blind man to see, a deaf person to hear, or a paralyzed person to walk. In God's power we can pray for the new limb or new organ to grow. Our Creator restores.

Ed, follower of Jesus and licensed clinical social worker

Discovering Emotional Well-Being

One goal of this book is to shed light on **what mental health is**, not just to describe illness. Below are positive traits of people whose souls are thriving because of their connection with the Creator.

Hyder's Five Principles for Maintaining Good Mental Health

Dr. Hyder, a Christian psychiatrist who practiced in New York City until his retirement, stressed health in all three aspects of the human being: body, soul, and spirit. His suggestion? One needs to relate well toward self, outwardly toward others, and upwardly toward God. These bullet points are a short and sweet description of mental health by O. Quentin Hyder, M.D.:[13]

- ❖ You accept that life isn't a bed of roses.

- ❖ You react to people in humble and loving ways.

- ❖ You develop a secure place in life.

- ❖ You settle on something to look forward to.

- ❖ You develop a strong personal faith that leads to practical action.

Koenig's Suggestions on How Religion Promotes Mental Health

In his work researching the benefits of faith on mental health, Dr. Harold G. Koenig suggested 10 ways that believing in God improves emotional well-being. He stated that his studies show that one's adherence to acceptable behaviors (as defined by the Judeo-Christian Scripture) actually promotes well-being. Religious doctrines, concerning good and bad behavior, place restrictions on one's lifestyle but produce general health. He

---

13 O. Quentin Hyder, *The Christian's Handbook of Psychiatry* (Old Tappan: Fleming H. Revell Co., 1971).

writes: "Religion both provides things and expects things in return. There is no free lunch."

The following is Dr. Koenig's list, presented as six benefits of faith. These compare similarly with Dr. Hyder's five principles for good mental health:[14]

- ❖ Faith promotes a positive worldview, helping to make sense out of difficult situations.

- ❖ Faith increases other-directness, enhances social support, and discourages maladaptive coping.

- ❖ Faith helps a person release a need for control and encourages forgiveness.

- ❖ Faith encourages thankfulness and an attitude-of-gratitude.

- ❖ Faith stimulates hope, which is the motivation toward health and healing.

- ❖ Faith gives a person a sense of significance with purpose and meaning to life.

---

14 Koenig, *Faith and Mental Health: Religious Resources for Healing*, 134-141.

3
THE VALUE OF LEARNING
THE NUTS AND BOLTS OF
MENTAL HEALTH

M Y SOUL SPRANG to life when I made my commitment to Jesus during my seventeenth year. I hummed with new purpose and sorted through questions more easily. But my conversion did not take all my emotional pain away, nor did it address all the injustices in the world around me.

A new question began to bother me:

Is there an enemy of a human being's soul—and is this evil enemy causing injustice and racism, war and murders, poverty and crime?

As I matured emotionally and spiritually, the reality of evil became more evident to me. I asked, "Were these psychological problems being orchestrated by some dark prince?"

During my four years of college (1964-1968), I did not receive an answer, although my soul grew in faith and knowledge. The Lord surrounded me with stable Christian friends and developed me spiritually through Bible study and prayer.

Experiencing the Landscape of Mental Illness

My first foray into mental health came in my junior year of college, when I chose to study the Negro Slave Personality for my thesis. That may seem a strange topic, but this was in 1966, only a decade *after* desegregation. Although in their eighties and nineties, the children of slaves who had lived on plantations were still alive and able to talk about their parents' experiences. Former slaves had left behind primary source material about coping with slavery. As I studied the institution of American slavery, I was heartbroken reading about man's inhumanity against man. I no longer doubted there was an enemy of man's soul. Slavery is forged from the pit of hell, undermines man's dignity, and destroys the soul's integrity.

From reading the testimonies of the 80+-year-old Negroes[15] who were children of slaves,[16] this was my conclusion: In order to survive slavery emotionally, a slave had to shape his personality in one of three ways. First, he could submit to the authority of his master and lose his sense of worth and *identity*. (**Identity** is defined as who a person experiences himself to be across relationships, situations, and time.) Second, the slave could be defiant and rebel against his master, break free, but end up beaten or lynched. Third, even while he was another man's property, the person could commit his soul to Jesus and find identity in God. My evidence for this last type of identity and spiritual freedom was found in the lyrics of Negro Slave spirituals.

After my college graduation, I received my license to teach high school history and took a position in a rural school. Right from the beginning, I discovered the intensity of emotional conflict within my pupils. They were rebellious, defiant youths, usually the children of uneducated farmhands and blue-collar workers. These teens had so many psychological problems that it was nearly impossible to teach them effectively. Their attention spans were short, and their behavioral outbursts were frequent. Unfortunately, their lifestyles included addictions, untimely pregnancies, delinquency, and truancy.

---

15 No offense is intended here. At the time of my thesis paper, this was a common term when referencing the time of slavery in the United States. I use the term only in reference to my paper's topic.

16 B. A. Botkin, ed., *Lay My Burden Down: A Folk History of Slavery* (Chicago: Phoenix Books, 1945).

But despite these mental health issues, these 15- and 16-year-olds had hungry souls. They often asked me questions about life and death, heaven and hell, God and Satan. I was careful not to mix their public education with my "religious views." For that reason, my husband and I chose to meet the youngsters in the village green for talks about spiritual matters. By the end of the school year, I decided that educating these children was going to be an uphill battle because of their emotional instability. So I left education for the field of mental health, taking a social work position at a state institution.

The Institutionalization of the Mentally Disabled

My next job was at a large state school for people with mental retardation, where I worked with "higher-functioning" women, although they were institutionalized and still "mentally retarded." (I am intentionally using 1969's vocabulary, although it is currently politically incorrect.) My job was to place the institutionalized females in newly created foster homes. Exposure to their institutional living environment changed me forever. I could see the presence of evil in and around me. The enemy of our souls permeates these institutions.

You may never see the inside of an asylum, so let me describe it. Behind the cement walls of *each* of the twelve block-type dormitories lived 160 human beings. Males and females of all ages had been dumped there because their "deficits" and "deformities" were too severe for them to function within their homes. They were "lifers," people who would die in that cement city. Each ward of 40 people was assigned two employees who had the responsibility for feeding, exercising, and disciplining these "inmates."

As I entered the asylum quadrant on my first day, I gasped at the horror. Three- to five-year-old children with hydrocephaly were sprawled out in individual cribs, row after row. Their skulls were as big as large watermelons, their atrophied bodies shriveled up to the size of babies. Able-bodied but "retarded" residents (not staff) cared for them. These "high-grade" women were assigned to clean up the "low-grade," cribbed children from their feces and urine, and to feed them as required. To do a clean-up, the "high-grade" women would spray the "moron" with cold water from a hose.

These ambulatory residents handled their own "calls of nature" by hiking up their smocks (no underwear) and doing their business right there on the floor. The day rooms reeked of urine, feces, and strong disinfectant. At times I had to plug my ears to their groans and screams, grunts and barks, all of which echoed against the cold walls. I had to breathe through my mouth, avert my eyes, and fight off tears when I first saw these people in such foul conditions. I was shocked that people had gotten away with caring for people with disabilities like this! I witnessed the enemy of our soul at work in the lives of these wounded people, foisting injustices on them, memories of which have stayed with me to this day.

One point of good news is this: Seven years after my work at that facility, the State of New York issued the Willowbrook Consent Decree, which identified similar horrific conditions.[17] In April 1975, the state government mandated a movement of the disabled into the community by placing them in group homes and foster care, a process called deinstitutionalization. While this change has brought some improvement, my observation of contemporary group homes (and prisons) reveals continued dehumanizing conditions.

Let me share the testimony of Kay, a lovely young lady who has been in ministry with me. She had an inside view of an "asylum" in 2007 because her mother placed Kay in a psychiatric hospital. When Kay was 22 years old, while living alone, she experienced a strange spiritual event. Her mother visited and saw

---

17 "Office for People With Developmental Disabilities," accessed May 22, 2019,

https://opwdd.ny.gov/opwdd_resources/willowbrook_class;

The Minnesota Governor's Council on Developmental Disabilities, accessed May 22, 2019,

https://mn.gov/mnddc/extra/wbrook/wbrook-timeline.htm.

her daughter beaten up and unable to speak. When her mother didn't understand that something spiritual had happened to Kay, she concluded that her daughter had a "mental" problem. So, she drove Kay to the psychiatric hospital and requested that she be admitted.

This institution was different from the New York State facility mentioned earlier because this place was for adults (not all ages) with normal intelligence (not mental retardation) who needed short-term stays (not a lifetime of care).

Kay's Testimony:
Eyewitness Account of a Soul Under Attack

In August of 2007, I spent a week in the psych ward, not because I had a mental health diagnosis but because I had a spiritual experience that was misunderstood.

Someone under the influence of evil had come into my home and had attacked me spiritually, mentally, and emotionally. What I mean by "under the influence of evil" is that this person was consciously and intentionally being used by the devil to bring destruction into my life. She left me beaten up and unable to speak, so when my mother called multiple times and couldn't reach me, Mom rushed to my home and found me in what she thought was a mental crisis. Immediately, not knowing what else to do, Mom drove me to the psychiatric hospital.

Upon my arrival at the institution and completion of initial paperwork, I was placed in the "emergency psych ward." This served as a temporary holding place until I could be transferred to the regular psych ward. I remember walking into that place and hearing a young man yelling from behind a door; he was in a padded cell. He was pleading with the nurse and kept saying, "I'm not crazy; I don't belong here." I felt a strong need to go over to the door and sing a song of peace to calm him. As soon as I began singing, he calmed down and stopped screaming.

Then the strangest thing happened: The nurse came over and said to the man, "John, it's time to take your medicine. You're hearing voices again." I looked at the nurse in disbelief and said to her, "Are you serious? You are making him think that my singing to him was his hearing voices. And you are going to medicate him further now?"

In righteous anger I immediately went over to the doctor and said, "These are God's people. Do you actually like manipulating and controlling other humans?"

He responded, "Maybe I do." The next thing I knew, two cops came around the corner and forcefully maneuvered me into my own padded cell. They body-slammed me and then injected a tranquilizer into my hip.

The next day I was taken over to the regular psych facility, where upon my entrance I read a sign on the wall that said: "No Prayer Allowed." As I was wheeled past rooms, I was saddened by the oppression I saw. One lady in particular was in her room, and the nurse had insisted on playing music for her that sounded as though it was from a horror film such as Silence of the Lambs. *The patient would literally yell, "help me," all day as the music was playing. Other patients were walking around like zombies. The nursing staff was very cold, unfeeling, and expressionless. I began to pray each night for freedom from oppression for each patient.*

At the time the staff admitted me to the facility, I had been able to hide a copy of my patient rights inside my gown during that short time. So when the doctor came in to visit me in my room, he was completely shocked when I pulled out my patient rights. He stammered nervously over his words. The next thing I knew I was being given Abilify and Depakote and was told I would need to take them because it was possible that I could have **Bipolar Disorder**. *Yet, I had never in my life struggled with manic behaviors.*

The side effects of the medications were horrible. I would be so fatigued and tired that I was almost in a zombie state. At night I would hear voices and have night terrors. Everything about the medication invoked fear and oppression.

As the days progressed, I continued to pray for those around me. Then something incredible began to happen! I was sitting in one of the support group sessions and one of the ladies spoke up: "You know, I am only in this facility because I was disobedient to the Lord. That opened a door for the enemy to come into my life."

Other people began to share. Before we knew it, a completely different set of staff was assigned to work the floor. One worker would sing gospel tunes during the support group sessions. A chaplain started coming and meeting with the residents and praying. One patient had his wife come visit him after a long period of their not seeing one another. And—get this: Remember the lady who would yell "help me" all day? The music was no longer being played in her room, and her right mind was restored!

The Bible says fear causes mental torment and anguish.[18] I witnessed exactly that while in the facility for seven days. But I also saw how God's perfect love cast fear out! By the time I left, everyone who was on the ward when I had arrived, had been released to go home.

Before I left, I was required to commit to meeting with the psychiatrist on staff once a month. After my second meeting, the psychiatrist released me. He verbalized that I had had a spiritual experience that "people just didn't understand." Now I wonder how many people out there have had the same situation happen to them: They have been labeled wrongly, being told that they have a mental health problem, while in truth they were undergoing a spiritual experience that was misunderstood.

Kay, 32-year-old social worker

---

18 1 John 4:18

Kay's stay in the psychiatric ward was due to her mother's misjudging what was happening within her daughter's soul and spirit. Her mother thought Kay's symptoms had an emotional cause. This story illustrates how important it is that we, as givers (even if we are just simple, caring people trying to help), have a rudimentary knowledge of mental health.

Understanding Defense Mechanisms: What We Use to Tolerate Soul Pain

One aspect of psychological problems I want to highlight is that of defense mechanisms, which are unconscious strategies used to cope with inner conflict. If a seeker wants to gain mental health, he needs to bring his defense mechanisms into consciousness so that self-awareness will help him change his behavior. Let me explain the importance of recognizing defense mechanisms.

Do you agree with this statement?

Every human being has the freedom to decide how he wishes to live.

Would you say "true" or "false" to that?

Free choice seems simple. However, often our wounded souls create barriers called defense mechanisms, which hinder sincere, truly "free" choices. So while we *should* be able to choose freely, often we develop unhealthy systems of defense against pain, which in turn block authentic responses. Any giver needs to discern defense mechanisms in the person he is helping. Likewise, any seeker needs to confront his defense mechanisms in order to gain health.

Because defense mechanisms are unconscious responses protecting a person from emotional pain, they can create a disconnect between our body, soul, and spirit. When this occurs, we do not know what is "truth" and what is a "lie." We also don't see ourselves as others see us. Defense mechanisms, created to help with pain, often make matters worse and cause additional injury. In one season of my life, I was blinded by the defense of **denial**, and this caused major problems, which I'll discuss later.

Psych 101:
Freud's Theory of Personality and Several Defense Mechanisms[19]

Sigmund Freud, an Austrian neurologist and the father of psychoanalysis, believed most mental processes were **unconscious.** *Specifically, the "unconscious" means that one's thoughts, feelings, and desires are functioning within the soul, although the person has no awareness of them. In Freud's* **Theory of Personality,** *psychological problems stem from unresolved conflict, which arises between unconscious sexual and aggressive impulses and society's rules and demands. The job of the defense mechanism is to manage the "unresolved conflict" so the pain can be tolerated.*

Freud taught a three-fold view of the human personality. According to Freud, the **Id** *is the instinctual center of the personality, where biological urges of aggression and sexuality rise up. The function of the Id is to help the person achieve pleasure and avoid pain, goading him to give into his desires and satisfy them. It operates from a strong need for immediate gratification (i.e., "I want what I want when I want it.").*

The **Superego,** *the moral component, represents the rule-based or societal demands placed on the person. The Superego's purpose is to police the Id and force the* **Ego** *to restrain impulses and conform to societal rules.*

The **Ego,** *the central part of the personality, handles all the battles between the Id and the Superego. To manage these internal conflicts, people develop* **defense mechanisms,** *unconscious actions that protect people from their emotional pain. All counselors should learn to recognize the defense of*

---

19 SparkNotes, ed., *Back to Basics Psychology, a Crash Course for People on the Go* (Sterling, 2014), 72-76.

> *denial; this is the refusal to acknowledge some behavior obvious to others. For example, an addict uses denial to ward off awareness of his habit and the painful feelings about his addiction, even when others are saying, "You are using too much."*
>
> *When you talk to a person who has little or no memory of her childhood, it is possible she is using the defense of dissociation. This means that unconsciously she has split off her trauma memories from her functioning ego, so they won't be brought to consciousness. But these buried memories will cause significant suffering. To be healed from the trauma, the patient needs to bring them to consciousness and to recover from them.*
>
> *Another defense mechanism is projection. This defense mechanism is operating when one attributes his own unacceptable thoughts, feelings, and memories to someone else. Clients who have had abusive and/or neglectful parents tend to project the negative traits of that parent onto God, a spouse, or their therapist. When working with a client, the therapist needs to answer this question: Has the person projected negative traits onto someone, thus hurting that relationship? Pointing these projections out to the person can increase his self-awareness.*

To help heal the wounds in a human being's soul, we need to understand **how people defend against their pain.** Some defense mechanisms may be healthy and appropriate. But at other times, they stymie one's emotional and spiritual growth. Givers should be helping seekers identify their dysfunctional defenses and replace them with functional ones.

I'd like to share three different stories illustrating **the defense mechanisms of projection, denial, dissociation, and repression.**

On Projection

I have had the privilege of traveling with Dr. Randy Clark and hearing his testimony, including how he used projection in a way that hindered his emotional well-being. To illustrate the defense mechanism of projection, Randy has permitted me to share a portion of his experience. This happened when he felt a spiritual disconnect from God because he projected his earthly father's personality onto his image of the heavenly Father. What Randy did happens to many of us.

Randy Clark's Testimony on Projection

In January 1994, I was faced with a call to go to Toronto [for ministry]. But I was scared that when I got to Toronto, God was not going to show up. I was afraid God wasn't going to use me. So I asked a friend for prayer, and the fire of God [term for the Holy Spirit] came upon me. But even after that, I still did not believe God would be there for me.

Why was this? I struggled with a lot of rejection issues. I was my own worst critic and was filled with self-doubt. My soul was injured. I was one really broken person. I had a dad who loved me, but he didn't know how to tell me that. When I was young, I vowed—if I ever had kids—I would tell my kids that I loved them. One reason I love the Holy Spirit is that when Dad was touched by the Spirit he'd start crying. Then he would motion for his kids to come over to him and say, "I love you." But as soon as he got [spiritually] sober again, he couldn't say it.

Here is how God healed me from this problem of projection. A few weeks before I went to Toronto, God had a Baptist businessman from Texas call to share a prophetic word with me. My friend said, "I have a word for you. The Lord says to you, 'Test me now. Test me now. Test me now. Do not be afraid. I will back you up. Do not become anxious because when you become anxious, you can't hear me.'" That prophetic word changed my life.

This Texas businessman didn't believe in prophecy. And actually, at the time, I didn't believe in prophecy either. But I believed the friend's word. That's why I think prophecy is so important because the power of prophecy changed my self-understanding and created faith within me.

My 12-year-old son, Josh, listening to me talk about Toronto, heard me say, "I hope God shows up." Josh responded: "Dad, you don't have any faith."

I said, "Son, I'm doing the best I can." That is the honest truth. I hoped God would show up. But I didn't believe He would. You see, I was projecting my experience with my earthly father onto my heavenly Father.

During my high school years, when I was playing sports, I would look up at the bleachers to see if Dad had made it to the game to be there for me. The problem was Dad worked so much that he wouldn't show up often. He worked for a union, and if they said, "Work," you'd work. The morning before the game, Dad would say to me, "Son, I want to be there." But more often than not, he wouldn't show up. While I knew he loved me, I couldn't depend on him being there.

Regarding the call to Toronto, I just didn't believe God would show up. When you think God may show up and you know He will show up, it makes all the difference in the world.

So in this situation, with my fear of what was going to happen and my question if God would use me, I knew what was wrong. I was projecting onto God my relationship with my Dad. There was such a deep-seated brokenness in me, that the truth about God never forsaking us was only in my thoughts, but it had not worked itself down into my gut.

That rhema word, the prophecy about "Test me now...I will show up," healed my brokenness. It reached in and repaired a defense mechanism I had lived with all my life. No longer would I project my fear Dad wouldn't show up. The Holy Spirit had brought healing to that wound of rejection, and I believed down deep that our very Big and Present God would be there and use me.

The next day, after I received that healing, I told my team we were going to Toronto, even though I had no idea what God was going to do. Our God is a God who does exceedingly abundantly above all that we ask or think. The Holy Spirit says, "Don't limit me." Thank God, He broke down my defense of projection.

Dr. Randy Clark, Founder and C.E.O. of Global Awakening (1994) and the Apostolic Network of Global Awakening (2008), which is dedicated to teaching, healing, and bringing impartation for revival to the nations

---

To illustrate the defense mechanisms of denial and dissociating, I share a patient's testimony. This lady displayed great courage as she opened up, confronted, and then wrestled with her trauma memories. Her therapeutic experience illustrates how a soul can become disconnected due to trauma, and then repaired through the healing touch of God.

Madelyn's Testimony:
A Lifetime of Using Denial and Dissociation

My doctor referred me to a psychologist because of chronic, lifelong difficulties with my intestinal tract and unresolved fibromyalgia. During the initial session, my therapist asked: "Have you ever been abused?"

"No," I said, "But I wonder because there were chunks of time from my childhood for which I have no memory." When we finished that first session, my therapist recommended I read the historical novel, White Heart,[20] *that she had written for people like me.*

---

20 Julie Caton, *White Heart: A Novel* (Mustang, OK: Tate Publishing, 2011).

I immersed myself in the account of a 17th century French-Canadian woman and saw in her character my own anxieties and confusion. She had been sexually abused as a teenager and had come to Canada to get away. She struggled with anxiety and was uncomfortable around men. Reading it shattered my denial about my sexual abuse. I had buried the horrible memories and set up emotional barriers. The stress of holding onto these toxins had created many physical ailments.

I was treated for Post Traumatic Stress Disorder. Because I was bringing the scary memories to consciousness, the treatment caused me to have nightmares and flashbacks. As a Christian, I had wanted to walk through my problems privately with just my Lord and Savior. But I came to realize that I needed professional help. I could not do this alone, and I needed encouragement to face the emotional pain as it surfaced. Thankfully, the psychologist incorporated Jesus and the power of His Holy Spirit into each session.

I pressed through a three-year, painful process in order to achieve the healing. Combining emotional with spiritual counseling gradually brought health. I can now praise the Lord for giving me a new beginning, a life filled with the joy of the Lord, and finally peace that passes all my understanding. The power of the Holy Spirit to heal (others as well as me) has been revealed to me repeatedly. Thank You, Lord.

Madelyn, over 60 years old, retired teacher

An Unnamed Child's Story: Her Preverbal Use of Repression

Emotions are packages of chemicals (formerly referred to as "**information substances**") stored throughout the body but most generally lodged in our gut. [See *Psych 101: Medication and Brain Anatomy*.] When trauma or emotional injury occur, a wound results, which is cellular damage stored in chemical form. For recovery to occur, the cellular damage needs to be identified and healed. Most of the time, either a faith-based counselor or a mental health therapist expects healing to result through "talk" therapy. But what does a therapist do if the patient can't or won't talk about a trauma because it occurred in her life before she developed sufficient speech to process the experience?

The answer: We use art or play therapy. When I worked at a residential treatment center for disturbed children, one seven-year-old girl became my patient. She was so disruptive, disorganized, and disrespectful that she could not be contained in the community, and was placed with us for residential care. The Department of Social Services had identified her since infancy as a child of an abusive and neglectful family.

Often, during our sessions, the child sat drawing pictures. One particular day, the first picture she drew was a typical one: a crayon drawing of a brown house, a girl in a pink dress, a tree with green leaves, and blue flowers under the yellow sun, which had a smiley face. When I asked her about her drawing, she said, "It's so pretty, isn't it?" Her response, and her colors and structure meant in child-talk: "I'm avoiding everything in my life that makes me sad and mad."

Then she drew a picture in black crayon: a tiny, stick-figure girl lay on a bed with a monster standing over her. When I asked her about that drawing, she said nothing and moved quickly away. She dove into the box of building blocks, and began to build and destroy towers, build and destroy, build and destroy.

After she went back to class, I looked at her psychiatric record and refreshed my recollection of her psychosocial history. At the age of 18 months, she had been sexually molested in her bedroom by her mother's boyfriend and then left alone while her mother went out. The child's mind had repressed that memory, but her body-soul-spirit connection had stored it. Because the event occurred before she had developed effective speech, she had never talked about the event. But here she was as a seven-year-old, with her memory brought up from the basement of her unconscious, ready to be "healed." And that drawing was the breakthrough in her getting well. Through therapy, using art and eventually words, she recovered and was placed in a healthy foster home.

My therapeutic approach has changed since I learned that defense mechanisms have their origin in emotions stored as a biological part of a person's make-up. Now I realize why my patients, those who have an abuse or trauma history, can't just "talk." Their emotions have penetrated not just their souls but their bodies and spirits as well. For this reason, I actively treat people as a **whole human being,** integrating **body-soul-spirit.** [Chapter 1 focused on this concept.]

Because emotional damage can affect one's body and spirit, as well as her thoughts and feelings (i.e., her soul), I share the testimony that follows. Please note, a psychological issue can cause a bodily pain (e.g., headache) or a compromised organ (e.g., digestive problems). To experience healing, we need to recognize the holistic system in which our emotions express themselves. The following testimony of Debbie, whose aching shoulder had bothered her for years, illustrates this. Because her husband chose his needs over hers, Debbie's emotional resources had run dry years ago, but she did not realize it. She had repressed the pain. For her, a primary breakthrough into greater health came when she forgave both herself and her husband.

Debbie's Testimony: Using the Defense of Emotional Repression

I was married to a narcissist for 25 years. But for the first 20 years, I did not have a name for the painful abuse my husband was dishing out. His need to make me his object and his failure to connect with me emotionally, hurt deeply.

About six years into the marriage, my right shoulder developed pain. I blamed it on the years I had served in the military and the excessive physical work I had done. As the chronic pain worsened, I sought traditional treatments, but these offered only temporary relief and negative side effects. Soon I noticed my pain levels increased as the oppression in my marriage escalated. When I was away from the toxic home environment, my pain would dissolve, only to return when I got back with my husband. Was this an example of the body-soul-spirit connection that I had read about?

Even though I was raised a Christian, I had never been taught that divine healing through Jesus was available in the 21st century. I was desperate and sought answers in spiritual healing. The message I heard was this: "Jesus Christ came to save people and heal them....Jesus was the same today as He was 2,000 years ago."

After I sought spiritual healing for many physical ailments, the chronic right shoulder pain continued. "Was there a spiritual block preventing its healing?" I asked myself. A few months later, a friend offered to pray. She laid hands on my shoulder and prayed for a few minutes. Then she looked up and asked, "Debbie, can you recall any specific injury to that shoulder?"

"Yes, I remember when my husband was teaching me about his new shotgun. He asked me to try it. I did. It had a terrible "kick" that he had not warned me about. I never sought medical treatment for that injury, and until now, I had forgotten about it."

When my friend prayed, she connected the physical "kick" of the weapon to the many "kicks" from my turbulent marriage. As she prayed, I saw not my shoulder but my heart. It was torn, bruised, and broken from being "kicked." I let my tears flow. That hour I saw the spiritual connection between the injured shoulder and the wounds of my heart.

This breakthrough allowed me to recognize something: My husband had not warned me about how his "kicks" might injure me. I was really angry about that. Unknowingly, I had harbored unforgiveness. When I asked the Lord to help me forgive him, I could feel warmth flow through me and my health return. Both my heart and my shoulder were healed under the power of Jesus's blood and God's grace.

Debbie G., age 51, homeschool mother of three children

Defense Mechanisms Reveal the Severity of Personality Disturbances

If we want to mend soul pain in people, we need to discern their defense mechanisms. Some of the defenses are common, easily identified and quickly changed, such as projection. Other defenses, seen less often, are hidden in the person's presentation, and are more stubborn when it comes to release and healing.

If you, as a giver, remain blind to your seeker's defenses, you may fail to help his emotional pain. The inner wound, which he is defending against, must be identified, then released as a necessary prerequisite for getting well. A physical illustration of this would be the onset of an infection in a body wound. Unless that original infection is treated, it will grow and fester, and the pain will worsen. A seeker needs to have the courage to let the giver "lance the boil," or clean out the putrefaction to overcome the problem.

A common example is the defense mechanism of denial in the presentation of an alcoholic. The giver can clearly see that the person drinks to excess and abuses alcohol (e.g., drinking a 12-pack per night), but the seeker still perceives that his beer drinking is not a problem. ("Oh, I only have a few each night.") Therefore, because the defense is in place, he is not motivated to change and has difficulty admitting the truth.

There are different levels of defense mechanisms:

- **Mild:** These are common and operate on the surface of the personality. We all have them, and they are healthy for the most part.
- **Moderate:** These are less common and embedded in the person, and may cause a variety of problems that need to be addressed.
- **Severe:** These are hardened, seriously dysfunctional, and largely unchangeable.

Likewise, there are three levels (mild, moderate, and severe) of personality structure or disturbances commonly seen in patients. These varied levels are caused by multiple factors, such as the person's preferred defense mechanisms, early family environment, and trauma history. I point out this distinction in the severity of personality types because a giver must assess the seeker's level of personality functioning. The approach the giver uses—e.g., the intensity of confrontation, perseverance, and limit-setting—should be influenced by whether the seeker's personality problems are mild (**stress response**), moderate (**personality disorder**), or severe (**psychotic**).

Psych 101:
Three Personality Types

In my opinion, there are three general categories of psychiatric diagnoses:

1) A person is having adjustment problems or a stress response following exposure to distressing situations, and is exhibiting mild symptomatic distress.[21]

2) A person is demonstrating an enduring pattern of behavior (i.e., a personality disorder) that deviates from the expectations of his culture.[22]

3) A person has a form of a psychotic disorder.[23]

One important distinguishing feature has to do with the quality of the person's perceptions of the world around them. A person (#1) who is enduring a stress response has a relatively healthy view of the world. His ability to interpret reality is similar to the majority of people around him. A person (#3) with a psychotic problem has a distorted view of the world. His interpretation of reality is seriously skewed and may not be rational; it may even be bizarre.

---

21 *Diagnostic and Statistical Manual of Mental Disorders* (Washington, DC: American Psychiatric Publishing, 2013), 812.

22 Ibid., 645.

23 Ibid., 87.

*He often appears grossly disorganized (or unique) in speech and/or behavior. A person who has a **personality disorder** (#2) lies somewhere in-between, on the borderline of two realities, with one foot in reality and the other foot in a psychotic thought process that is uniquely his. This person is very changeable, inflexible, and difficult to manage.*

Because of these differences, the quality of communication varies. Someone with an adjustment problem is usually easy to communicate with. Once his defense mechanisms are identified and released, counseling can be productive. Someone with a psychotic problem struggles with adequate communication. He will fail to engage in a reasonable discussion because his perception of reality (which is poor) and your perception of reality (which is normal) are entirely different. Someone with borderline traits shifts between rational communication with normal perceptions at one time, and an emotionally volatile presentation due to a distorted worldview at another time. He is stable for a while but then becomes very upset and irrational, and then switches back again. His character appears "disordered." When a giver recognizes these three types of people, he can understand the potential or limitations of helping a specific seeker.

4
TENSIONS THAT ARISE IN THE LANDSCAPE OF MENTAL HEALTH

B ASIC AWARENESS OF the nuts and bolts of the human personality, especially how defense mechanisms shape one's behavior, creates improved teamwork between the scientific, mental health community and the supernaturally inclined, faith-based community. In my effort to bridge the chasm between the two, this chapter will focus on some areas of tension spawned out of skepticism, misunderstanding, and distrust.

Tension With a Pastor Over Misunderstanding the Biological Need for Medication

Medication is a common "solution" to mental illness, but it is often misunderstood. Do you know the prevalence of medication used for depression and anxiety? In the United States, the use of antidepressants has increased 400 percent in the last two decades.[24] That means at least 13 percent of the adult population in the United States takes antidepressants. A giver should be familiar with this information and not urge someone to go off his medication; this is dangerous. Any medication changes need to take place under physician supervision.

---

24 Janice Wood, "Antidepressant Use Up 400 Percent in US," *Psych Central*, August 08, 2018,

accessed October 6, 2018, https://psychcentral.com/news/2011/10/25/antidepressant-use-up-400-

percent-in-us/30677.html.

I have met some well-intended Bible-believing pastors who have had false impressions about medication. One Sunday morning, I gasped while listening to a pastor's words. This elderly minister ran his hand over his opened Bible, and said, "I know some of you in the congregation are feeling a little down. You may even be depressed. Others of you are troubled with worry. I'll bet you're taking medicine for anxiety. But let me tell you: If you would just turn back to the Lord, He will take care of your depression. If you would just trust the Lord more, He will clear away your anxiety. You won't need your pills." As he peered over his glasses at the 120 parishioners in the room, my hands clenched. My heart ached.

Blood rushed to my face. Why? A few rows in front of me sat a lady I was treating for depression, a mature Christian woman who loved the Lord. To my left, sliding down in his seat was a young man, a new believer, who was dealing with anxiety. And they were both on appropriate medication! What could I say to them or to the pastor? My silence was not helpful.

So I decided to share my concerns. After the service, I asked if the pastor could spare me some time. I described the biological nature of psychiatric disorders and why people use medication. Thankfully he was open to my comments about psychological issues being similar to physical illnesses—and not a "sin." He received the information I share in *Psych 101: Medication and Brain Anatomy*. The following week, from the pulpit, he apologized for his error in handling mental illness the way he did.

Recently, an industrial engineer came to see me because he was burned out from his demanding job, felt emotionally flat, and couldn't express his feelings. He sat on my couch, bowed over his knees, and wrung his hands. He said, "I shouldn't have emotional problems. Right? I'm a Christian, after all. I must not be in a right relationship with the Lord. What is wrong with me? How have I sinned?"

His physician put him on an antidepressant; the patient was relieved to hear his problems had a biological source. The next week, I said, "What you are feeling is not the product of your 'lack of faith,' or any specific 'sin.' This is a chemical imbalance, like an illness, affecting all areas of your life. It's like this: You are moving through life wearing a metaphorical pair of glasses, with the lenses tinted 'depressed.' They influence how you interpret everything, including your relationship with God. You see everything negatively, including your faith walk. This perspective does not result from something you have done. It's the depression speaking. Why don't you suspend your feelings a while until you get better?" Later he reported this conversation had unburdened him and had given him new understanding about the nature of clinical depression.

The information in *Psych 101: Medication and Brain Anatomy* is important, not just for pastors and teachers, but for seekers as well. Many people take medication simply because their doctors tell them to. They often don't know what their pill is doing to their brain or even what their doctor's credentials are.

Psych 101:
Medication and Brain Anatomy

Medication for mental health problems is usually prescribed by a psychiatrist (M.D. with psychiatric residency training), but sometimes by the primary care doctor (M.D., D.O., or nurse practitioner). If the patient is being treated by a psychologist (Ph.D. or Psy.D.) or social worker (LCSW), that therapist would need to refer his patient to a prescribing physician.

Our brain, a two-hemisphere, egg-shaped glob of gray tofu-looking matter, is made up of billions of brain cells called neurons. Under the microscope, these neurons vary in shape, have a center (soma), axons which carry signals to downstream neurons, and branches (dendrites), which stretch out in all directions. One neuron comes close to touching another, and that second one almost touches the third one. The display is like trees with branches reaching out toward the next tree. Along these brain cells' branches, electrical impulses flow as though traveling along a highway carrying signals.

Notice I said the neurons come "close to touching." They never touch because the electricity in one would "short-circuit" the other one. So there are gaps between the branches called synaptic gaps. Neurotransmitters are stored in the axon terminals. Think of the chemicals as little ferryboats carrying the signals (that came down from the dendrite's electricity) over the "river" of the synaptic gap to the next nerve cell. On the "shoreline" of the nerve cells there are "docks" for the ferry, called receptor sites.

Psychiatric medications *manage a person's symptoms by regulating the amount and type of chemicals in the synaptic gap by changing the neurotransmitters to a healthy level. Medication side effects may result because of the person's incompatibility between the medication and the receptor sites. So, doctors make adjustments as needed.*

More than 30 years ago, Dr. Candace Pert researched our emotions and concluded that the brain is a bag of chemicals (once called "information substances"), and the chemicals are widespread, not just moving through the brain but through the entire body.[25] Today, we know that emotions and memories are definitely stored in the brain, generally as changes in the relative strengths of connections between neurons.[26] For example, studies show that some deeper parts of the brain (that is, the amygdala, the hippocampus, and the medial prefrontal cortex) represent emotional memories, among other things.

Research using neuro-imaging techniques has shown that key brain systems, which are linked together, have problems with emotional reactivity, notably in the study of Post-Traumatic

25 Candace Pert, *Molecules of Emotion: The Science Behind Mind-Body Medicine* (New York: Scribner, 1997), 141.

26 Personal Correspondence with Dr. Joshua Brown, Professor of Psychology and Brain Sciences at Indiana University.

Stress Disorder (PTSD). Specifically, the amygdala responds with greater activation to emotions induced by trauma. The medial prefrontal cortex appears to undergo changes when trauma occurs. This part of the brain is volumetrically smaller and shows reduced sensitivity to emotional states. In addition, the hippocampus, which interacts with the amygdala when encoding emotional memories, shows a decrease in volume.

Contemporary research in neuro-anatomy also reveals that what you think about does have long-term effects within your brain. For example, in a study of the experience of gratitude, imaging showed that there were positive changes when the subject was experiencing gratitude.[27] These overall findings regarding our brain functioning suggest the marvelous complexity of the human brain and the profound interconnection between our emotional experiences and what goes on inside our head. For an excellent sermon on how our thinking changes our brain, I recommend Bethel Church's Pastor Kris Vallotton's "Learning to Think."[28]

Tension Because of People With Atypical Brain Functioning

It helps givers to know that mental problems are not caused by the "sin" or character flaws of a person, but can result from neurodevelopmental difficulties. While about 95 percent of the population is "neuro-typical," meaning their brain structure and interior design are within normal range, about 5 percent are not.[29] Genetics, brain injuries (including prenatal ones), and

---

27 Prathik Kini et al., "The Effects of Gratitude Expression on Neural Activity," NeuroImage 128 (January 1, 2016), accessed February 28, 2019, doi:10.1016/j.neuroimage.2015.12.040.

28 Kris Vallotton, "Learning to Think," Kris Vallotton's Podcast (audio blog), December 21, 2018, accessed April 8, 2019, https://podcasts.apple.com/us/podcast/learning-to-think/id158029989?i=1000426309532.

29 *Diagnostic and Statistical Manual of Mental Disorders*, 61.

environmental toxins can cause these neurodevelopmental issues.[30]

People with abnormal brain functioning might have the diagnosis of **Attention Deficit Hyperactivity Disorder (ADHD)** and may contend with a brain overloaded from stimuli, such as their own thoughts, emotional reactions, bodily sensations, and "noise" from the environment. Their brains lack a good filtering system. Their brain cells, which should be functioning to block incoming stimulation, are not doing their job optimally. People with ADHD may become bored easily, act/speak out impulsively, create crises, and tend to be disorganized. Many people with ADHD indulge in overwork and compulsive behaviors, always having to keep on the move in order to feel "normal" and avoid feeling bored.

Brain problems can cause a person to have certain traits that place them diagnostically as having **Autism Spectrum Disorder (ASD).** People with ASD have neurodevelopmental problems resulting in social and emotional deficits. People with traits of ASD are characterized by persistent problems in social communication and repetitive behaviors. They may be insensitive to social cues, display emotional inflexibility, and struggle with abnormal social perceptions. Many fail to develop a "theory of mind,"[31] which means they don't have empathy for others; they are unable to "stand in the other person's shoes" and see things from the alternative perspective. As a result, people with ASD tend to be black-and-white thinkers, unable to compromise, and often struggle with functioning in school and at jobs. Children with similar characteristics used to be diagnosed with **Asperger's Syndrome (AS)**; it is technically no longer a diagnosis on its own but is now part of a broader category under **ASD.**

---

30 Sungji Ha et al., "Characteristics of Brains in Autism Spectrum Disorder: Structure, Function and Connectivity across the Lifespan," Experimental Neurobiology, December 2015, accessed June 05, 2019, https://www.ncbi.nlm.nih.gov/pmc/articles/PMC4688328/.

31 "Theory of Mind," Wikipedia, December 15, 2007, accessed June 05, 2019, https://en.wikipedia.org/wiki/Theory_of_Mind.

Whatever the causes of a person's emotional problems, the good news is that these can be healed. Healing can come from our medical/psychiatric community and/or from the power of God through inner healing.

Tension Within Our Social Environment

Thus far, we see how a complex set of variables weaves into the tapestry of a person's emotional issues. Genetics, chemical imbalances, neuroanatomical differences, personality structure, and **defense mechanisms** all play a role in establishing good mental health. An additional influence in a person's psychology is his/her home environment. The first five years of a child's life are the formative years, the time when the child's personality is shaped.[32] The degree to which he accomplishes the following three fundamental tasks will influence the rest of his life: learning to trust, achieving a sense of autonomy, and taking initiative while free of guilt. If the child fails at these developmental assignments, he will have chronic problems with mistrust, shame, and guilt, respectively. Healthy home and school environments are the key to a child's success. When a giver assesses how well a seeker has mastered these tasks, he will greatly increase his understanding of the seeker's psychological problems.

As we move through our typical day in the western hemisphere, statistics suggest that we may be in proximity to a person with a mental health problem and not realize it. That person may be working hard to appear symptom-free and somewhat normal. Whether we are in a grocery store, riding on an airplane, or sitting in a church, there is a high probability someone with mental illness is in that same locale with us. Soul pain is much more prevalent than we may realize.

---

32 Selma H. Fraiberg, *The Magic Years: Understanding and Handling the Problems of Early Childhood* (New York: Scribner, 1959).

Tension Over Judgmental Attitudes

I often hear complaints from new clients that they did not like their previous counselor. When these seekers explain "why," they report feeling misunderstood, or judged, by their giver. Sadly, the seekers are usually referring to someone pastoring them in the church setting. I hear criticisms about faith-based counselors being "judgmental" more often than the trained mental health workers. Why might this be?

During their schooling for mental health careers, givers in this field are trained to practice a nonjudgmental attitude toward their seekers. In contrast, people counseling within the church setting often have not received training on how to do this. Two important clinical techniques that a graduate of any counseling program must be skilled in are:

- How to relate to the seeker with "**unconditional positive regard**"
- How to maintain a **nonjudgmental attitude** while in the role as a giver

Attitude #1:
Practice Unconditional Positive Regard

Unconditional positive regard is a classic term taught to counselors; it may well be the most important skill people in the field of mental health can share with the faith community. *Unconditional positive regard* means the giver completely accepts and regards the seeker with no conditions attached. Carl Rogers, one of the most well known psychologists, coined the term in the middle of the 20th century.[33]

Rogers had experienced a conversion to Christianity as a young man. He came to respect this style Jesus demonstrated: that of accepting His fellow man with no strings attached. Dr. Rogers

---

33 Carl R. Rogers, *On Becoming a Person* (Boston: Houghton Mifflin, 1961).

started attending a theological seminary[34] but became disillusioned with academics and switched to child guidance. He concluded that real therapy began when people, motivated to achieve inner wholeness and health, worked out their problems in the presence of an accepting, nonjudgmental human being, namely the therapist.

Rogers anchored his client-centered therapy on humanistic beliefs. Humanism is the philosophy that declares people are basically good. Rogers believed God's divine love for us was unconditional. He viewed the nature of man the way God did at the moment the human being was created. That is, man has been created in the image of God, and therefore he is very good (Genesis 1:26).

To be an effective giver, we need to practice *unconditional positive regard*. However, if we settle on the doctrine that man is basically good (as did Carl Rogers), problems arise because that belief contradicts God's truth. Jesus taught this biblical doctrine: Mankind, originally created as good, fell into sin. Human beings are sinners, no matter how "good" we appear. During His ministry, Jesus told us people were evil at their core. "For out of the heart come evil thoughts—murder, adultery, sexual immorality, theft, false testimony, slander."[35] Jesus also said, "No one is good—except God alone."[36]

The concept of "sin" is hard for us to accept. Perhaps another word similar to sin, but easier to understand, is "iniquity." According to Bob Sorge, "iniquity is the evil bent of the human heart, that capacity within all of us to sin, that cavernous dark side of our hearts…and the ugly things that arise that we don't fully understand."[37]

---

34 Daniel Goleman, "Carl Rogers, Leader in Therapy, Dies," *The New York Times*, February 6, 1987.

35 Matthew 15:19

36 Mark 10:18

37 Bob Sorge, *Pain, Perplexity and Promotion: A Prophetic Interpretation of the Book of Job* (Grandview: Oasis House, 2015), 74.

The word for "sin" in Greek (*hamartia*)[38] means "missing of the mark." It is the same as this word picture: an archer draws his arrow back, shoots, and then misses his target. Within each person we have a natural tendency to miss our targets, particularly the goals of true goodness and complete love. That biblical view contradicts the idea that man is innately virtuous. If we go along with Carl Rogers and believe in the inherent goodness of man, we may face a problem and be unable to find the root cause of a seeker's issue. The iniquity within the wounded soul has to be taken care of in order to bring healing.

So, how should we handle a seeker's "sin?" This is what I've chosen to do: I relate to my seekers in their **pre-fall state**, loving them as God does originally. I position myself to look beyond the wounded person's behavior and to see him as "good," even while I believe the doctrine, which says there is sin in his spiritual core. This viewpoint is possible because of Jesus's sacrifice on the cross, which erased the confessing person's sin. I hold an unconditional, positive regard toward the seeker, while at the same time asking God to reveal the "iniquity" within him that is blocking his mental health.

Attitude #2:
Practice a Judgment-Free Counseling Relationship

This next comment may be hard to believe: I have learned more about how to accept people unconditionally from my secular, humanistic teachers than from anyone else. During the time I was a psychology student, I observed nonbelieving counselors treating their patients, and I witnessed more love and acceptance than I've seen in many faith-based workers over the years. In my experience, mental health workers (who admit they do not live from a faith perspective) are much less judgmental of negative behavior than church-based givers. Sadly, the latter

---

38 W. E. Vine, *Vines Expository Dictionary of Old & New Testament Words* (Nashville, TN: T. Nelson Publishers, 1997), 1045.

group has their antennae up for "sin" and how people "fall short," which they often tactlessly address.

Why are these scientifically trained clinicians successful in relating to their patients with a nonjudgmental attitude? *Because secular programs train students that way.* The counseling supervisors watch their trainees closely, looking for any way the psychology student may be inserting her opinion about the client into the therapy process. We are taught to embrace the positive in people, while managing (without judgment) the negative.

The following vignette offers an example from my training. When I was a first-year doctoral student, my supervisor viewed one of my mandatory videotaped sessions. In it, I am sitting across from a young college student, listening to her. She is seated on a couch. Between us is a table with a vase of flowers and a box of tissues. As she tells me how guilty she feels for having had a recent abortion, she chokes up. Her sobbing continues. Within a minute, I reach for the tissue box and hand her one. She wipes her tears away. The conversation goes on, and the session ends.

Later when my supervisor reviewed this with me, she asked: "Why did you give her a tissue?"

"Because she was crying and her nose was dripping," I said, somewhat puzzled.

"Was that tissue something *she* wanted? Or did you hand it to her because *you* were uncomfortable?" My supervisor paused, letting me search out that answer. I squirmed under her gaze.

She continued, "What message did you convey to her by doing that? Perhaps she wanted to keep crying. When you handed her the tissue were you suggesting she was wrong to be crying? Or were you saying, 'Hey, time's up, enough crying now—*I'm* becoming uncomfortable'?"

I share this experience because many givers do not have the training or the discipline to withhold subtle judgments. Often givers respond from the place of their own religious (or otherwise) expectations and personal needs; they end up inadvertently judging the person, as I did.

Seekers tell me how embarrassed they have become when their pastors speak in certain ways. For example, one of my clients told her pastor she was grieving from a recent abortion. His response? To give her a pro-life lecture. She was so uncomfortable that she walked out of his office in tears. Why had the pastor failed to hear her heart? What were his motives behind the pro-life lecture? If he thought about it, would he even recognize his error and then demonstrate genuine understanding and forgiveness the next time?

Possible Causes of Being Judgmental

Suspending judgment during a session is important. Therefore, I would like to share **possible causes** of why some of us judge others with insensitivity. Often, while we are filled with faith and want to love the seeker as Jesus did, our propensity for judging others still rears its ugly head. I know I have to monitor myself.

What are the psychological variables causing such a judgmental attitude? One reason behind our judgment might be that **we don't know Jesus all that well**. Perhaps we have a misconception that Jesus loaded people down with moral and religious rules, and we should do the same.

So, how did He respond to sin? Jesus certainly did not have an attitude of "anything goes." He did not condone immoral behavior or sinful thought processes. Through all, however, He continued to love the person. As an example, let's look at how Jesus dealt with the woman caught in adultery.[39] The religious leaders brought her to Jesus, expecting Him to condemn her so they could kill her. They said something along the lines of, "She's caught in the very act. Under our law, she should be stoned."

---

39 John 8:2-11

What did Jesus do? He *contained* the situation. He stepped down and wrote something on the ground. He used God-given wisdom to say, "Let any one of you who is without sin be the first to throw a stone at her."

He *waited patiently for His spoken words* to register. After the men dropped their stones and walked away, Jesus rose from his kneeling position in front of the adulteress and said, "Then *neither do I condemn you....*Go now and leave your life of sin" (emphasis mine).

He accepted her. He loved her. There is no time in which Jesus approached people with the attitude they had to change in order to be loved. *He loved them first,* even in the face of their sin. He loved them *before* they changed. In fact, His love *motivated* their change.

Our fear may be the second possible reason we are judgmental. Perhaps our faith is weak, and we're scared the other guy, this "sinner," will attack our beliefs or tempt us away from obeying God. Maybe we are afraid that if we "accept" the sinner's sin, we will somehow be tainted? So, we react to our fears by clinging to the rules of our religion. We become rigid and pharisaical.

Many western churches are exclusive and not inclusive. Even though churchgoing people follow Jesus—and know that Jesus did not come to judge the world but to save the world[40]— they still shun the people who are living alternative lifestyles. Such behavior of exclusiveness might be observed as a blatant act, like glaring at "sinners" or whispering about them behind their backs. Or, the shunning could be subtle, such as a coldness and unwillingness to embrace people with their hangovers, multiple piercings, or same-sex partners. What exactly is the problem? Are church counselors afraid of "different"? I believe "different" does not mean "bad"; it just means *different*.

---

40 John 12:47

These "different" people are my clients/seekers. [And I am one among many.] We are people who seek out counseling because we are struggling with interpersonal relationships, immoral choices, illegal consequences, addictions, phobias, and brokenness. Often we are living "alternative" lifestyles because of our mental health problems. An example is the homeless veteran struggling with PTSD, unable to function and living on the street. Another example is a young woman who may cope with her history of childhood sexual abuse by choosing a same-sex partner or even multiple partners.

A third factor causing a judgmental attitude is **our ignorance**: Some Christians don't know what to do with people who are "different." Often, faith-based people are not knowledgeable about supports that might help those in alternative lifestyles. Givers should develop a list of contacts, trustworthy people, or agencies that can provide resources to people in need, no matter how "different" they are.

Strategies to Overcome Negative Attitudes

As a therapist and a Christ follower, I'd like to share some **basic strategies** used to overcome my own innate tendencies to be judgmental.

1. The **first step** is saying the old adage: "There but by the **grace of God** go I."

I recall the messes and bad choices I have made, and I recognize how God's love has rescued me. Because He is my model when it comes to the temptation to judge others, I try to maintain a closer walk with Jesus. I ask God to help me live—based not on *my* own faith—but operating from *the faith of God in me*, His gift to me.[41] Using God's faith allows me to not fear *my* faith being shaken, since the true faith operating is not mine really, but God's. In His faith, I have put on the protective armor

---

41 Ephesians 2:8

70

of God,[42] so I'm not afraid of being tainted by the other person's sin. I use the *faith of God* to turn on the faucet of God's love. It is by God's grace His love runs through me.

2. Second, I hold to this promise: The **Holy Spirit is the one who has the job of convicting us.**[43]

If people are to recognize their sin and feel guilty about it, their heart must make a spiritual shift. This only happens by the intervention of the Spirit of God (Holy Spirit) and the Word of God, not anything I say or do. "Convicting" others is not our job, but rather God's.

3. Third, I consider what Jesus said: "The very words I have spoken will condemn [the disobedient] *at the last day*" (emphasis mine).[44] **We do not know the whole story** or God's plan for the lives of other people.

We cannot presume to understand people's hearts or personal histories. If we fall into judging them, we are making assumptions about them that are none of our business. People's souls are God's responsibility, not ours.

I wanted to understand how an attitude of non-judgment is conveyed to patients, so I reached out to a former client. Karen and I had started a counseling relationship 18 months earlier because she had been struggling with depression and anxiety, perhaps due to stress on the job and her father's deteriorating health. She was discontent despite the fact she was successful in her career, active on various sports teams, and happily married to her wife of eight years. We acknowledged our differences about the Christian faith (in which she was raised but currently questioning) and moral choices (one being same-sex marriage). We worked well together, and when she recovered from PTSD due to sexual abuse in her childhood, she was discharged. At our

---

42 Ephesians 6:11

43 John 16:8

44 John 12:48

last session she thanked me and said, "I really appreciate the fact you weren't judgmental."

Her comment interested me. After several weeks, I called and asked, "At our last session you said you didn't feel judged being here, talking to me. And yet with previous counselors, you had felt judged? And we even had different beliefs, right? How could that be?"

"May I think about that?" she asked. A day later, Karen sent me this email.

Karen's Response About "Judging"

People in therapy routinely expose a vulnerable part of themselves. Being able to talk through one's most sensitive thoughts and feelings without fear of judgment is paramount. Talk therapy isn't a doctor treating a physical ailment, like setting a broken bone and letting the body heal from an illness. The patient is taking part in her own treatment this time. If patients feel as though they are being judged, regardless of how many times the therapist may say "you can be open and honest with me," they simply won't.

For you and me, that was never a problem. You skipped the part where you lectured me on the semantics of "everything is safe here" and went straight to opening yourself up to me instead. That was why I felt safe talking to you. Not because you said it was, but because you showed me it was. I don't know if doctors typically do that, but it was a powerful gesture. "How could I think this woman is at all judgmental when she's being open about herself with me?" Your transparency made all the difference moving forward. Hope this helps!
—Karen

An effective giver must maintain a nonjudgmental attitude and establish an environment of *unconditional positive regard* while knowing the extent of the "sin" in the client's life. I encourage an untrained counselor to seek out some form of clinical supervision. Hopefully, knowledge of these tendencies discussed here, coupled with self-awareness, will stop any giver from conveying judgment inappropriately. All givers need to turn to the Holy Spirit for help, so we can love the seekers the way Christ loved them.

Karen's observation—that of maintaining an attitude of transparency—is critical if two people are going to respect each other and communicate effectively while they are viewing the world from two different perspectives. My desire for open disclosure is at the heart of this book. As I unpack the toolboxes of both science and faith, I want people to share the gold treasures—some coming from the mental health information base and some derived from the faith community. In addition, with transparency, I expose how I personally have explored the topic of soul pain. My desire has been to create a strategy for overcoming this pain, which I call the psychology of suffering

Tension Between Science and Faith

During my early training, I gained head knowledge. But what I learned had little effect on my heart and soul. I perceived an underlying tension that hummed like a sour musical note in the background throughout my process of discovery. I could not comprehend what it was at first. Within a short time, I discovered it stemmed from the rift between science and faith.

By this point in my journey, I had stopped working in the institution and had enrolled in a social work school to learn more about this problem of the disconnected soul. I was both a new Christian and a new student of "mental illness." Shortly, the clash between psychology and faith jolted me and left me challenged both intellectually and spiritually.

This was 1970. I discovered that for the past century, animosity had grown between psychology and religion. These opposing schools of thought considered their opponent a cult and became suspicious of each other. Thirty years previously, Sigmund Freud poured fuel on the fire when he labeled religion a crutch that people used to deal with their helplessness. He said the idea of God came from one's need for an idyllic father figure; religious beliefs were simply illusions.[45]

My newly formed worldview was becoming a composite of science and faith. The social work program was based on the science of psychology. The instructors trained me in psychoanalysis, a method which relied on the concept of the unconscious. We learned Freudian techniques, in which the use of the "unconscious" was popular. Freud taught that the unconscious consisted of repressed memories, once held in our consciousness, but pushed down and bothering us. He popularized the belief that religious people should set aside their faith in God in favor of science.

While I attended this program, most of my Christian friends were skeptical of my choice of profession and did not hold to the scientific worldview. I had to fend off their criticisms, particularly my husband's, as the religious community declared Freud's teachings "heresies." While I was taking courses, my husband argued against anything of or pertaining to psychoanalysis and the unconscious. He believed no one but God—no therapist or counselor—should "meddle" with a person's soul. To him, if the teachings were not faith-based, and the counseling techniques not supported by the Bible, they were not acceptable.

As you can imagine, tension arose in our marriage.

My husband Rex and I met through a Christian campus fellowship group in 1966 and were married upon my graduation from Smith College in 1968. We were new converts, passionate about **sharing the Lord** and serving people for Jesus's sake. At the time, secular culture supported the view that a woman was educated and polished for the purpose of supporting her husband and his endeavors, not her own. Similarly, our Christian culture

---

45 GotQuestions.org, "Is Faith in God a Crutch?" GotQuestions.org, March 23, 2010, accessed May 22, 2019, http://www.gotquestions.org/faith-God-crutch.html.

maintained the belief that men should lead the church, while women should live in quietness and submission and not assume authority over men. My husband was in full agreement with these power differentials between male and female.

So, when Rex told me it was not God's will for me to continue my studies, I barely questioned him. I asked meekly, "Why do you say that?"

He said, "Because they are teaching about the unconscious, which is not a scientifically proven fact. It certainly doesn't show up in the Bible. What goes on in one's soul is God's business, not some unbelieving counselor's." Under pressure from him, with my weak-willed acceptance of the husband's right to interpret God's will for his wife, I withdrew from the program.

PART TWO:

BRIDGING THE DIVIDE
BETWEEN TWO LANDSCAPES

5
TWO BRIDGES CREATE A LINK BETWEEN SCIENCE AND FAITH

Bridge One:
A Psychology of Suffering

HAVING BEEN PROPELLED from childhood to help others, it comes as no surprise that, as I entered my married life and career path in mental health, I wanted to figure out soul pain. Before I was actively studying to be a social worker in 1970, my mother had placed in my hands a small booklet entitled *The Presence of God*, a collection of messages, written by her uncle, Brother Allan Whittemore, an Episcopal monk and former missionary to Liberia. My great uncle, "Pudge" as we called him, had been the Brother Superior to the Order of the Holy Cross in West Park, New York, until his death in 1960. One of his messages was on the need to create a "psychology of religion." He stated that religion and psychology had one common goal: helping brothers and sisters manage their suffering. He challenged his readers to discover a psychology of suffering.

It wasn't until recently, as I was going through my personal library accumulated over 50 years, that I came upon his little book. I realized Uncle Pudge's idea to formulate a psychology of suffering was key to helping people with their soul pain. Brother Whittemore said that the domain of psychology, based on the rational thinking of the mid-20th century, and the domain of religion, based on the supernatural thinking of his Christian tenets, were the two primary fields addressing man's suffering. Neither group did it well, he bemoaned; each landscape had something to offer, so combining the two would be ideal. But he left that task to the next generation. The conclusion of my book focuses on this important bridge—the psychology of suffering—but I will save this best for last.

Bridge Two:
Science Proves the Value of Faith in Healing

In the last four decades, researchers have declared that faith is important in healing. In 1990, the American Psychological Association stated: "The religiosity of an individual must be addressed within clinical practice."[46] A year later the *International Journal for the Psychology of Religion* began to publish articles on the intersection of religion and mental health. One of the founding reasons for this journal was to help out pastors because they were looking to psychology and the related mental health disciplines for insights to guide them in pastoral care.[47]

Scientific studies now support the benefit of faith when it is part of the healing process. This well-researched finding is a natural bridge between the mental health community, which desires wellness, and the faith-based community, which teaches the doctrine of faith. Therefore, the second of the four bridges is just this: Science has proven that faith is valuable in one's healing process.

What Is Faith, Religion, and Spirituality?

By now you know faith is important to me on a personal level and that science has shown that the faith of individuals can

---

46 Edward P. Shafranske, ed., *Religion and the Clinical Practice of Psychology* (Washington, DC: American Psychological Association, 1996).

47 Stanton L. Jones, "A Constructive Relationship For Religion with the Science and Profession of Psychology; Perhaps The Boldest Model Yet," in *Religion and the Clinical Practice of Psychology*, ed. Edward P. Shafranske (Washington, DC: American Psychological Association, 1996), 113-47.

aid in the healing process. So let me ask you: Is your faith important *to* you?

What is *faith* really? The dictionary says faith is belief that is not based on proof. The Bible says, "Now faith is confidence in what we hope for and assurance about what we do not see."[48] God's Word also tells us faith is what makes us right with God.[49] From my experience, faith is the inner conviction I've had that propels me to step toward God. Once I take that step, I gain the spiritual awareness that God is real and active, even though my five senses can't prove it.

In 2015, faith became even more important to me because of a miraculous healing. So I began to study how faith impacts the health of people. Through Dr. Randy Clark, I was introduced to the research of psychiatrist Harold Koenig, M.D., at Duke University. I also met Andrew Newberg, M.D., from the University of Pennsylvania[50] and read the writings of psychologist Kenneth Pargament, Ph.D.,[51] from Bowling Green State University. Along with others, these three experts are investigating the impact of religion, religiosity, and spirituality on people's health. They are discovering the presence of spiritual/religious experiences within the brain functioning of human beings. Scientific journals are stating: "Faith can be extremely helpful in the healing process."[52]

While a description of research methodology goes way beyond the scope of this book, I offer several important facts.

---

48 Hebrews 11:1

49 Philippians 3:9

50 Andrew Newberg, Eugene D'Aguili, and Vince Rause, *Why God Won't Go Away: Brain Science and the Biology of Belief* (New York: Ballantine Books, 2001).

51 Kenneth I. Pargament, *Spiritually Integrated Psychotherapy: Understanding and Addressing the Sacred* (New York: Guilford Press, 2007).

52 Richard Besser, "Is Religion Good for Your Health?" ABC News, March 25, 2013, accessed May 22, 2019, https://abcnews.go.com/blogs/health/2013/03/25/is-religion-good-for-your-health/.

These researchers, committed to rational thought, are looking for answers to completely "irrational" questions. In order to do this, they must clearly state their hypotheses (i.e., the questions they are trying to answer) and define their terms. Their research focuses on questions such as:

- Does faith in God enhance one's physical and emotional health?
- Was the human being created to worship God?
- Does God's presence in one's brain change its neuroanatomy?

Once the question is stated, the researchers form consistent definitions of words such as "faith," "spirituality," and "religion." "Religion" or "religiosity" is a term describing a person's commitment to a belief system and his participation in an institution connected to that belief. Religion includes the practice of prayer, rituals (such as baptism and communion), and fellowship (the assembling of the group); each of these is an outward demonstration of behavior. The practice of religion may or may not be connected to a spiritual belief or inner faith.

Spirituality is quite different from religion. If a person is "spiritual," he is sensitive to his inner soul and the spiritual energy in the world around him. This spiritual energy may or may not be emanating from Jesus.

For the researchers cited above, the word "faith" refers to a variety of belief systems. For the purpose of my writing, I am using "faith" as a very specific term—faith in Jesus Christ as the Son of God. Here, faith includes the precepts of the Old and New Testaments: There is One Supreme God who became flesh in Jesus and sacrificed His life to bring grace to mankind. When I use the word "Christian," I am referring to a person who has had an **encounter with the Living Christ** and has surrendered his or her life to Jesus.

Another term I've been using is "faith-based." For my purposes, a faith-based person is someone who is committed to Jesus and born spiritually through the power of the Holy Spirit. I am a faith-based person. I might even call myself a faith-filled person. But I am also religious because I participate in a church body (congregation) and enjoy the rituals. I am also spiritual because I believe we live in a world that has spiritual energy circulating: good energy under the authority of Jesus and evil energy under the domain of Satan.

What Is the Science of Faith?

People are fascinated when they consider the possible connection between any faith and one's **brain anatomy. Neuro-theology** is a discipline of study focusing on that connection.[53] Neuro-theologians argue that the human brain predisposes us to believe in God. They say deep inside the cerebral cortex (i.e., exterior part of the brain) is the limbic system buried at the brain's base and incorporating the emotional core—the hypothalamus, amygdala, and hippocampus. Studies have shown that these brain structures are "activated" when people are praying or worshipping. Researchers argue that there must be a neural imperative for man to believe in God because thinking about God changes the way in which the brain operates.

Research has confirmed that faith plays significant roles in people's lives and that this explains why religion doesn't go away over time. In studies done by Newberg and Lee, the "God brain" (i.e., the limbic system) shows evidence of mystical states, a sense of the subjective experience of God.[54] So, if the human brain was wired for faith, it stands to reason that faith promotes man's physical and emotional health.

This has been confirmed: More than 90 percent of Americans believe in God or a higher power. About 70 percent pray on a daily basis. Forty percent attend a church or synagogue regularly. Eighty-two percent acknowledge a personal need for

---

53 Newberg, D'Aquili, and Rause, *Why God Won't Go Away: Brain Science and the Biology of Belief.*

54 Bruce Y. Lee and Andrew B. Newberg, *Religion and Health: A Review and Critical Analysis.* Zygon, Vol. 40, no. 2, June 2005, University of Pennsylvania, 444.

spiritual growth.[55] Based on these statistics, it behooves us to incorporate spiritual resources into the healing process.

Considerations in Teaching the Importance of Faith

Given the conclusions from two decades of research about the value of faith in the healing process, psychologists and psychiatrists may have underestimated the power of religion in the lives of their patients. Perhaps, these scientifically minded practitioners—as a group—tend to be far less religious than the patients with whom they work. Because of the research that is being done, there is a change coming. Dr. Koenig told me that medical and psychological training programs now recognize the importance of spiritual resources as a necessary ingredient in one's healing processes. Students who are currently enrolled in medical and nursing schools, social work, and counseling programs all agree about the need to incorporate "faith" into the healing models.

Recently, I visited The Christ Hospital Health Network in Cincinnati, Ohio, because of my interest in faith and healing. The Network has included a "spiritual assessment questionnaire" in its electronic medical record. Upon admission and each day of one inpatient stay, the nursing staff engage the patients in discussions of their spiritual needs and supports for care. The Network also has started a certificate program for medical professionals and faith community representatives through its School for Healing Ministries, with the goal of offering biblically informed healing prayer to its patients.[56]

Research has made it clear that spiritually sensitive care enhances patient satisfaction. Patients report that they like to know where their care provider stands spiritually and to create a

---

55 "World Religion News Articles 2018: Religious News Stories Blog," World Religion News, accessed May 22, 2019, http://www.worldreligionnews.com/.

56 For more information, contact Chaplain Doug Mitchell at doug.mitchell@thechristhospital.com.

positive connection with their doctor by praying together. Patients want to talk about how their faith (of any kind) is helping them during their illness. The more life-threatening the medical problem, the more important this openness about faith becomes. When a patient is facing death and is receiving comfort from his belief in God, he likes to share his faith with his caregivers.

So those are the scientific findings. But **how do we incorporate faith-based discussions into our counseling sessions?** When I worked at the community mental health center, I was apprehensive about being transparent about my faith. One reason for cautiousness had to do with the longstanding principle that government agencies should not be involved with religion (i.e., maintaining the "separation of church and state"). Another reason was that the staff members were unenthusiastic about faith and did not discuss spiritual matters. Statistics reveal that only 40 percent to 45 percent of mental health practitioners believe in God (37 percent of psychiatrists).[57] As I talked to colleagues, I discovered that the nonreligious therapists never brought up the subject of faith—even if the patient dropped a hint.

So here's the question: **Does the therapists' reluctance to open a discussion on faith hinder the quality of their patients' recovery?**

Research shows that it is important for the patients to talk about their spiritual lives. If you agree the answer is "yes," then we should introduce faith in the process of healing.

I hope that the following section on including faith issues in counseling sessions is helpful.

The Importance of Discovering One's Spiritual Core

If we believe faith is valuable in the pursuit of greater health, then that path of discovery starts with knowing one's

---

57 Joseph A. Califano, Jr., "Religion, Science and Substance Abuse," *America, The Jesuit Review*, Feburary 11, 2002, accessed May 22, 2019, https://www.americamagazine.org/issue/360/article/.

spiritual core. Since the time I worked on my psychology degree in 1985, I've given this question a lot of thought:

What is the nature of man and his spiritual core? Particularly, is there a spiritual root to his emotional problems?

These questions were the focus of a term paper I wrote. I was taking the course in order to test the waters of this doctoral program and to prove myself a worthy candidate for admission.

The well-established, scientifically oriented Jewish professor gave us this assignment: "Write a paper on what you believe about the nature of man, the source of mental illness, and the best therapeutic intervention?" I debated how to handle that assignment. Should I be forthright, given my position as a **born-again Christian** attending this high-end secular university? Or should I respond to the assignment in the politically correct way? The latter response would help my chances of being accepted into the program. Yet, if I selected the former answer, I would remain true to myself.

The term paper stated my three answers. I took a big risk because my opinions contradicted the "acceptable" responses:

1. Where the science of psychology presumes man is basically good, I stated that man was created good but fell into a sinful state.

2. Where the psychologists deduced mental illness is the result of chemical imbalances and/or poor family structure, I stated that man's fallen nature (including mental diseases and poor moral choices) comes from the original core of humanity's sin.

3. Where most clinicians concluded that healing derives from a therapeutic relationship with a good counselor, I stated that *complete* healing needs to go beyond that. For a person to discover his identity as a healthy human being—i.e., to become fully human—one needs to know God personally.

Opening Up Conversations About Faith and Soul Pain

I believe one's spirit is as important to the person's health as is his body or his soul. Because of that, I routinely ask my patients about their spiritual resources. Since I am in private practice (thus, not government-funded), I have the freedom to question seekers about their spiritual lives. Given the increase we see in research findings that religion is proven to be beneficial to healing, more therapists might want to consider adding this question at first contact: **"What are your spiritual resources?"** Dr. Koenig's staff takes a spiritual inventory of their patients at the time of their intake.

Do you know what a mental health intake questionnaire looks like? The patients are peppered with questions in order to fill out the insurance-mandated intake form and to provide context for the counselor. The questions include:

- Name, age, occupation?
- What brings you here?
- What symptoms do you have?
- Are you on medication?
- History of drugs or alcohol?
- Previous counseling?
- Birth or family trauma?
- History of abuse?

And finally, I have added: "What are your spiritual resources?"

To that question, about one-third of my seekers answer without blinking an eye: "Ah, I go to church." Or, "I believe in God. Why do you ask?" "Oh, yeah, I'm a Christian." But these people don't offer much more. With this group, I push for more information: Are they praying people? Do they find reading the Bible worthwhile? Do they have a personal relationship with Jesus?

The other two-thirds stare at me with baffled looks. I pause, waiting for them to think it through. The adults stumble around with vague answers, like "Ah, I'm not sure." "Is there a right answer?" Usually the un-churched teens don't understand the question at all.

So, I offer them an answer: "Spiritual resources? They are the parts of you that connect with God. Or if you don't believe in God, it's the part that helps you experience beauty or love or gratitude. Do you have any idea now?"

Their answers become a platform from which I will build a strategy to introduce them to their spiritual selves. My heart's desire is that they will come to realize they have a spirit and that this spirit yearns to be awakened by the love of Jesus. A person's emotional self cannot achieve wellness until he or she is connected to the Creator. After all, the Creator made the person, knows every hair on his head, and knows every injury to his soul. Who better than the Creator to participate in the healing of this person?

Listen Well, and Watch for an Entry Point

Here are some suggestions for tapping into the spiritual side of your seeker. A skilled mental health worker, tuned to hear what her patient is saying, may well discover an open door to faith issues. For example, if my seeker said something like: "I feel I let God down," I would capture that comment, not letting it slide by. I might ask gently, "Oh? What do you mean? I'd like to hear more."

Sometimes you can pick up a cue, not so much from what the patient is saying, but from what she is doing. You might notice the seeker is rubbing her necklace, on which is a cross or an angel. Or a teen might be wearing a t-shirt with a key phrase or popular saying on it. These "nonverbals" can also be entry points into further discussion.

Use Open-Ended Questions

Another client might say: "I'll never forgive myself for that." In response, I might inquire: "You are having trouble forgiving? What could God do to help?"

Please notice how open-ended that last question is. If the patient shut me down, I would resume "traditional" counseling etiquette—"don't discuss religion." However, if the seeker began to talk about his shame or fear of God not forgiving him, I would gently lead him into a conversation to shed light on his spiritual position.

I would ask: "What are your thoughts about God? Do you believe God loves you? Does the God in whom you believe have a heart to forgive you?"

Assess the Seeker's Spiritual Resources

Seekers may not realize what their spiritual resources are. Many don't know that they have both a soul *and* a spirit. They don't realize these parts of them need to be recognized and cared for. Explaining about the triune body-soul-spirit can be a good place to start. Perhaps opening up the broad topic of "spirituality" will help. Our human spirit, that part wanting to connect with the Divine Spirit, is what we feel as we enjoy walking in natural beauty or listening to a symphony. The Bible says, "[God] has also set eternity in the human heart."[58] Isn't it our jobs to tap into that resource?

Perhaps seekers have recollections from early church experiences but don't see how this is applicable to their current lives. They may not understand Christian doctrine, or, if they know about Jesus, they may not know how to apply faith in Jesus to their situation. Jesus says that if we lift Him up so people can get to know Him personally, He will draw them to Himself.[59]

We need to help seekers discover that God wants to be involved in bringing wholeness into their lives. We can point out ways in which we see God working in their lives. We can question whether or not they are holding onto erroneous beliefs that are blocking their healing. Does their upbringing offer any

---

58 Ecclesiastes 3:11

59 John 12:32

building blocks to help them walk in faith? At a minimum *we do not want to leave the seekers ignorant of their spiritual potential.*

Don't Shy Away From Mentioning God as Part of the Solution

Many seekers believe in God.[60] Regardless of where each seeker stands spiritually speaking, anyone who enters counseling is struggling with some emotional issue. With that in mind, we can freely inquire whether or not they have thought about involving God in their problem. Would they agree they are not receiving sufficient help from God? Would they like to ask God to step in? Possibly, they have not even thought to ask for divine help. Assure them that it is God's desire to provide care and comfort.

---

60 Frank Newport, "Most Americans Still Believe in God," Gallup.com, June 29, 2016, accessed May 22, 2019, https://news.gallup.com/poll/193271/americans-believe-god.aspx.

6
BRIDGE THREE:
COMMON PRACTICES USED WITHIN
BOTH MENTAL HEALTH AND FAITH

A NOTHER BRIDGE BETWEEN the landscapes of science and faith is the common practices they share. Psychology and faith have been thought to be incompatible because science is objective and quantifiable, and religion is subjective, qualitative, and unmeasurable. Despite their differences, there is a fundamental similarity between the two. Each field grapples with the human experience and attempts to make sense out of the complex existence of the human being.

Beyond that singular idea, I thought about what else psychology and faith have in common. The following seven practices are recommended by both the scientific, mental health community and the supernaturally driven, faith-based community.

The Need to Express Emotions

Givers—both trained mental health workers and people counseling within the model of Jesus's ministry—follow this unique advice: It is important to express how you feel. Jesus emphasized this value when He taught that one must "become like little children" to enter the kingdom of God.[61] This is another way of saying: Enjoy your feelings. You are an emotional being. Look at the child who laughs and cries without pretense. Be like

---

61 Matthew 18:3

him. Mark Baker wrote: "Vulnerability and emotional spontaneity are important in developing good mental health."[62] This principle is best modeled by people who have the heart of a child.

The Confessional as a Helpful Tool

Another practice shared by both sides of our "bridge" is that of the **"confessional."** A confessional is a place where a seeker can sit with a giver and "unload" what is on his heart. It's a safe setting, free of judgment, where one can speak out the problem and receive understanding and emotional relief. The place of the "confessional" may vary from the therapist's couch to the priest's closet to the pastor's office, or even a table at the nearest coffee shop. But in each situation, the person is offered the space and time to unload his problems. The spoken word holds healing power.

When the seeker says, "I'm sorry. I did/feel _____," and the giver says, "I understand and accept you as you are," healing occurs.

Earlier we looked more at this ingredient of "judgment-free" counseling. Practitioners in both fields should convey a nonjudgmental attitude toward seekers.

Self-Awareness as an Essential Goal

A third practice is the encouragement of a seeker to become **"self-aware."** Knowledge of self is foundational for both maintaining emotional stability and/or growing in one's faith. An ancient Greek sage wrote, "Know thyself." Jesus said, "The truth will set you free."[63]

To be self-aware means that you know who you are. The cornerstone of a healthy personality structure is a clear sense of

---

62 Mark W. Baker, *Jesus: The Greatest Therapist Who Ever Lived* (New York: HarperOne, 2007).

63 John 8:32

identity. Here, the person has a stable sense of who she is over time, places, and circumstances. When a person fails to have a firm identity, she has lost an anchor to help her with mood swings or irrational thinking. Therefore, it is an important goal for either the psychologist or the pastor to aid the seeker in "finding herself."

Self-awareness is particularly important for a seeker who is volatile and irrational. This type of personality was the research topic of my doctoral dissertation. Evidence shows that a person with a **Borderline Personality Disorder (BPD)** has one primary flaw in her personality—that of a lack of stable identity. Hence, one's achieving a strong sense of personal identity is critical for her mental health.

While self-awareness per se is an important clinical goal, it is not easy to achieve. People don't like to look at themselves. Take the fairytale *Beauty and the Beast* as an example. For the Beast to be transformed back into the Prince that he was created to be, he needed to face the monster within. This process of "facing the monster," or letting the truth about oneself set you free, is more easily accomplished when the seeker has a trusting relationship with the giver. Therefore, my treatment recommendation is to encourage the patient with BPD to form a relationship with Jesus and to be transformed by the Holy Spirit. People with BPD can be difficult to relate to, so partnering with God gives this person a loving, consistent, heavenly Father to be her persevering, all-loving therapist.

Let me introduce Lynn, a middle-aged woman who struggled with mental health issues for many years until she "found herself." When she wrote her testimony of healing, I asked her if she had been given the diagnosis of Borderline Personality Disorder, and she said, "yes."

Lynn's Testimony: Finding My Identity in Jesus

At the age of 35, when I was diagnosed with multiple mental problems, I was very angry with God. Having been raised in a Pentecostal Church I had tried to live for Him, but failed. My young adulthood was messed up with rebellion, rage, **eating disorders**, and addictions. I had no sense of who I was. My thoughts were filled with statements of self-rejection, condemnation, and defeat. These undiagnosed illnesses plagued me. [Eventually, I learned that I had a Borderline Personality Disorder.]

I did not know until later that these mental problems were inherited from my relatives. From the outside, my mother and father appeared to be "very successful," but they had a variety of emotional problems. The doctors tried me on every psychotropic drug cocktail to stop my torment of mental illness. I put myself into a variety of therapies three days a week. But the torment continued, so I went back to self-medicating, and I decided to end my life. At that point, I admitted myself into the "best hospital in the nation," but it wasn't helping. Even though the staff saw me as high-risk for suicide, I finagled a way to go home, more hopeless than ever.

Several months later, my cousin invited me to go see a "healer." Once there, I prayed at the altar but then erupted into a rage. I screamed, "Just show me any person Jesus has healed!" The hostess gave me a card with the address of the nearby healing room. Weeks later, I was there, filling out the form and admitting that I was suicidal, addicted, and bipolar.

A woman walking through the office door stopped and said, "Jesus told me you were coming." With that, the prayer staff led me into the sanctuary, put on the song "Sit With You Awhile," and the lyrics spoke to my heart. I felt the power of Jesus's presence. This was the beginning of my total inner healing.

I continued to visit small groups of praying people who told me I was listening to lies, but I gave them a hard time.

They would say, "The devil is a liar."

"But I've always been like this," I'd challenged.

They'd say, "You heard that voice because you are being lied to." They'd repeat God's truths over me time and time again. "He loves you, Lynn. You are special to Him. He is a God in the business of healing brokenness."

The lies began to fall off as I listened to Jesus's teaching, heard worship music, and read about Jesus. I was 100 percent consumed with being with Him. For decades I had not known who I was. Now, I knew that I was a beloved child of God. My identity was in Jesus. The power of the Holy Spirit transformed me from the inside out.

Lynn Eldridge, Minister of the Gospel of Jesus Christ, Real Estate Investor

---

In the case of Lynn, her self-awareness helped her discover God. When her soul was invaded by the Spirit of Jesus Christ, Lynn's personality transformed. Whether a wounded soul has the diagnosis of BPD or not, the Spirit of the Living God is the powerful ingredient generating change and giving the person mental health. Where loneliness and hopelessness are present, God's Spirit provides love and hope. Where chaos and instability are rampant, God's Spirit stabilizes the person's emotions. When a person suffers from a fragmented soul, as Lynn did, connecting that soul to the Spirit of the Creator brings emotional freedom.

Pursuing Healthy Relationships

Another area of common ground between secular and religious givers is their goal of helping seekers build **healthy relationships**. We all desire quality connections with people because well-adjusted bonds teach us to **self-soothe**. In Lynn's case, her emotional instability and erratic behavior drove her in and out of harmful relationships. Only after she linked herself with Jesus and had Him as her primary "go-to," did her personality begin to normalize. This was the point at which she learned to self-soothe.

Human beings are relational organisms. We people like people. We were created to have a healthy dependency on other people. Both psychological theory and spiritual doctrine have this in common: A human being has an inner call to connect to others. The Lord God said, "It is not good for the man to be alone. I will make a helper suitable for him."[64] We were created to be dependent on God and fellow man, and within these relationships, we become whole.

One reason dependency on another human being is important is this: Healthy, dependent relationships teach us to regulate our thoughts and feelings in a process called "self-soothing." Self-soothing is the tool acquired when a baby forms a healthy parent-child bond, which carries him into adulthood. Either a therapeutic relationship and/or a connection with the Holy Spirit is the ideal classroom for learning to self-soothe, perchance that skill is late in developing or needs improvement. Father God is the best teacher of self-soothing. Here's an applicable Bible verse: "When worries threaten to overwhelm me, [God's] soothing touch makes me happy."[65]

---

64 Genesis 2:18

65 Psalm 94:19, New English Translation

Psych 101:
The Importance of Self-Soothing

Here is the process to achieve self-soothing: A loving caregiver, ever-present in an infant's life, picks up and cares for the frantic baby and calms him down. Thus, the infant is "soothed." Over time, the maturing child learns to do that soothing for himself. In adulthood, we soothe ourselves in the activity of caring for others, as well as in managing ourselves.

If problems arise, people often seek to soothe themselves in unhealthy ways. When relationships don't work, they shift their reliance off that key person and become dependent on "things." They turn to drugs, sex, food, money, media, etc., in an effort to self-soothe.

When a seeker attaches to an object (i.e., something to do the soothing), the giver may discern that a breakdown has occurred in the seeker's mental health. In psychological terms, the object is their addiction. In spiritual terms, the object has become an idol. An addiction or an idol is a false, inanimate "god" that the person relies on for security and contentment. This object does not satisfy, and one's reliance on that "idol" is a one-way street to negative emotional symptoms.

To repair this unhealthy behavior, the person needs to connect with the living Spirit of God instead of with the "dead" object. Inanimate objects are a toxic substitute for this connection with the True God. We were created by God to be loved—and soothed—by Him. God is the One who is meant to do the soothing, and connection with Him is the key to healthy relationships.

Practicing Meditation Brings Focus

Meditation is a pastime encouraged by both secular counselors and believers of the Bible. Methods of meditation have one practice in common, according to Dr. Candy Brown: "[During meditation] one pays attention in a particular way...in the present moment...resulting in the goal of stress-reduction."[66] Because meditation is a strategy used in both the mental health field and the faith-based community, I would like the readers to understand the fundamental differences and distinct benefits of these two types of meditation. In both cases, their benefit is relaxation of the soul. However, it is important to highlight their differences.

The discipline of meditation in Buddhism and other Eastern religions emphasizes the practice of emptying one's head of all things. In this process, one centers on his own body or breath, and achieves mindfulness by focusing on a mantra. In contrast, Christian meditation focuses, not on emptiness, but on the Almighty God, the One who gives the source of life and breath. Early Christian monastic practices emphasized contemplation, a simple, thoughtful, slow reading of the Bible, which is one form of meditation. Bob Sorge recommends meditating like this: Practice "pressing into God's word, and unlocking the hidden riches of Scripture."[67]

Bethel Church's pastor, Beni Johnson, writes about the benefits of meditation in her book on being an effective prayer intercessor:

> I know when I am really in that place where I feel completely connected to God because I have an instant peace.... It is almost saying 'aahhh' in my spirit, soul, and body.... I become much more aware of how it feels when I have lost that connection.... When I allow His presence to consume me, I surrender myself so completely to His will that my desires begin to line up with His.[68]

In the Judeo-Christian tradition, the first suggestion "to meditate" was spoken by Jehovah God to Moses's successor,

---

66 Candy Gunther Brown, *The Healing Gods: Complementary and Alternative Medicine in Christian America* (New York: Oxford University Press, 2013), 38.

67 Bob Sorge, *Secrets of the Secret Place: Keys to Igniting Your Personal Time With God* (Kansas City: Oasis House, 2001), 72.

68 Beni Johnson, *The Happy Intercessor* (Shippensburg: Destiny Image, 2009), 165-169.

Joshua.[69] The Lord said, "The Book of the Law shall not depart from your mouth, but you shall meditate on it day and night…so that you will make your way prosperous and then you will have success." The Hebrew word for meditate means "to muse or mutter, or chew the cud." Chewing the cud is the best visual for the process of meditation in the Judeo-Christian culture. A cow bites into her food and chews, swallows, and regurgitates, at least three times. The chewed food goes into one of her stomachs, where it is processed, and becomes sweeter as she repeats her "chewing of the cud." I experience the benefit of meditation when I "bite off" some of the Word of God, chew on it, and let it enter my gut. There it is digested and becomes sweeter and more nutritious with each "cud."

The term "mindfulness" comes out of Buddhism, a belief system that focuses on the relief of suffering.[70] Other non-Christian meditation styles also aim for the practitioner to relieve pain by gaining unity with the divine. Please notice that in both of these descriptions of Eastern meditation, the underlying assumption is this: Through emptying one's mind and focusing on his own divinity, the human being is elevated to equality with God. Before I had read Dr. Brown's work, I had not realized this, and it troubled me. Why? Because that goal—focusing on my divinity—sounded like the original sin. In the story of the fall of mankind, the enemy used similar words to tempt Eve: "[If you eat the apple]…you will be like God, knowing good and evil."[71]

The Eastern view teaches that the person meditating will arrive at knowing he is one with God. On the other hand, the Christian view believes that "oneness"—reconciliation between the individual and Father God—is only possible through the atoning death and resurrection of the sinless Jesus Christ. For me, it is important to know what I'm doing and why, since I don't want to be practicing a behavior that is not aligned with God's

---

69 Joshua 1:8

70 Brown, *The Healing Gods,* 39.

71 Genesis 3:5

will for me. When I meditate, I want to maintain spiritual purity and position my heart to be devoted solely to Jesus.

Journaling Clarifies the Issue

Journaling is another technique that I have recommended to my clients and use myself. When one is in the process of sorting out inner pain, taking time to write out your burdens and anger, as well as your blessings and praises, can relieve that emotional pain. Givers in both the mental health field and the community of faith suggest it to seekers as a beneficial therapeutic outlet.

Recently, a participant in one of my classes on the psychology of suffering asked me, "I can see that your time with Jesus helps you deal with life's pains. How do you achieve that intimacy?" Among other strategies, I suggest journaling.

Have a pen and paper within reach, and silence your environment—no phones, no crying babies, no distracting music. Shift into a meditative mode, and open your soul by inviting the Spirit of God to partner with you. Praise the heavenly Father, and thank Jesus for what He has done for you. Make sure you have repented of any known disobedience. Then, focus on what you want to say and what the Lord is saying to you. Start writing. Silence your inner critic.

For this exercise to be successful, you must believe that the Holy Spirit lives within you and that the Spirit of Jesus talks to you. To build up your understanding, read through John 13-17. Develop a deeper awareness of how the Holy Spirit operates within you, offering you knowledge about the heavenly Father and His kingdom (as the Spirit did to Jesus). The source of this flow of ideas is the Word of God, "the food" you need to feed your soul at another time. With that being said, jot down the ideas the Holy Spirit gives you. Don't critique yourself at this point because you can reflect on what is written later and hold it up to the standard of the Word of God.

To enliven this experience, add the practice of two-way journaling. Believing that you and God are speaking to each other, write down a concern or question you have for Abba Father. Perhaps write something as simple as: "How can I know You better?" Then *listen*. Write down the Holy Spirit's response. Keep pressing in to that style of communication until your heart feels satisfied. As you grow in the Word, this journaling exercise becomes very powerful.

Storytelling Enlivens the Counseling Process

Storytelling, sharing tales from one's life and giving **testimonies,** are favorite practices in both types of counseling. The common ground of telling personal stories helps us to discover the truth about ourselves and about others. The process of sharing experiences and encouraging hope refreshes us.

Stories move us away from hard "head knowledge" and into what we feel. Jesus used parables "to force us to deal with what we believe rather than what we think we know."[72] Jesus rarely lectured; instead, He used real-life examples to bring home important concepts. As people listened to His stories, they had to open their ears and dig a little deeper in order to personalize the heart lessons that Jesus offered.

Our testimonies serve several purposes:

- We like to hear how other people fight their battles and win, so stories keep us alert.
- They educate us about options we haven't considered. Learning what worked for "Susie" may help someone find a solution to her own mental illness.
- Testimonies spread the good news of Jesus—a soul saved, a healing, a deliverance.
- When words of success get out, people find that their faith increases.
- Most importantly, our stories defeat the enemy of our soul. The Apostle John wrote: "They triumphed over him

---

72 Baker, *Jesus: The Greatest Therapist Who Ever Lived,* 4.

[Satan] by the blood of the Lamb *and by the word of their testimony…."*[73]

---

73 Revelation 12:11, emphasis mine

7
BRIDGE FOUR:
COUNSELING WISDOM DERIVED
FROM JESUS

J ESUS'S SERMON ON the Mount is the well-known message
spoken by the Carpenter from Nazareth, when He addressed
more than 5,000 men, plus women and children.[74] The "mount"
was an expansive elevation above the shores of the Sea of
Galilee. This section of the Gospels is also called "the
Beatitudes," which means a list of attitudes that bring happiness.
Jesus made suggestions for living well that are so similar to
principles taught in counseling schools, I've wondered if the
founders of therapy techniques were influenced by this Man of
God. What are these radical but basic principles for psychological
health? I have selected nine to highlight.

Change Your Thinking...and Be Blessed!

The first radical idea Jesus offered is this: To live well, one
needs to think differently about life. At the onset of His ministry,
Jesus declared: **"Repent, for the kingdom of heaven has come
near."**[75] In modern language, this means: "Change your
perspective because God's kingdom is here." These words are
similar to what therapists say: "To achieve good mental health,
you need to think differently." Or they may suggest, "to reduce
your suffering and gain full health, you might want to try thinking
God's way."

---

74 Matthew 5 and 6

75 Matthew 4:17

In therapy, we often use the technique of "reframing." Reframing, in essence, is rethinking or repenting. This means we help the seekers find positive ways of interpreting situations, relationships, or attitudes. Dr. Pargament studied the behaviors of subjects who are more religiously committed and found that they are more likely to reframe negative events as opportunities to grow than their less committed counterparts.[76]

The root cause of mental illness may result from a fundamental, internal conflict that occurs when we human beings straddle two perspectives—the negative and the positive, or man's and God's. While we live in both our physical world and in God's spiritual realm, these two ways of living have different rules and viewpoints. Each of these "realms" has a different headship. Our earthly existence is under the regime of darkness, decay, and death. Its power source is the evil one; Satan rules it. However, our spiritual realm is under the domain of Holy God. Its power source is the Heavenly Father; God reigns there.

These two truths mean that we human beings experience a dual existence: earthly and materialistic on one plane, and spiritual and divine on another. How confusing! This is where our stress comes from. For us to benefit from Jesus's principle— "Repent, for the kingdom of God is here"—we need to decide where to place our allegiance. Jesus said that we cannot serve both God and mammon (i.e., worldly wealth and/or corrupted desires).[77]

How does this dichotomy affect one's mental health? I see us positioned on the center line in a spiritual tug-of-war, pulling toward earth or pulling toward heaven at different times. Could this duality be at the heart of one's mental illness? When a person straddles this line, his soul is subject to a real inner battle, split

---

76 Kenneth I. Pargament, "Religious Methods of Coping: Resources for the Conservation and Transformation of Significance," *Religion and the Clinical Practice of Psychology*, ed. Edward P. Shafranske (Washington, DC: American Psychological Association, 1996), 215-239.

77 Matthew 6:24

into two. He can't have it both ways. Chronic indecision alone creates stress. The Apostle James wrote: "Such a person is double-minded and unstable in all they do."[78] Every human being has to decide where he is going to plant his feet, spiritually speaking: in God's kingdom or in Satan's domain?

Mental health problems, such as mood instability and psychoses, have their origin in this confusion. For a person to gain emotional freedom and come into a season of mental health, he needs to rethink his life choices. By what set of rules is he going to play: God's or man's?

Throughout the Bible, God has outlined healthy values for successful living. When we adhere to them, we have a foundation for good psychological development. Four thousand years ago, God gave mankind a moral code called the Ten Commandments.[79] When we obey this Law, our bodies and souls are protected from decay and corruption. However, despite our best intentions, we make poor choices. Yet, for the mistakes we do make, God offers us a solution. It is found in the death and shed blood of Jesus.[80] When we rethink our choices, embrace God's plan for living, and receive the gift of Jesus as Savior, we are empowered to disconnect from spiritual darkness. Making these positive choices that are aligned with the Creator will help people discover resources for their mental health.

Admit Your Spiritual Poverty...and Be Blessed!

The second radical idea Jesus shares is this: **"Blessed are the poor in spirit, for theirs is the kingdom of heaven."**[81] One biblical paraphrase is: "You're blessed when you're at the end of your rope." To be blessed means someone is carefree, cheerful,

---

78 James 1:8

79 Deuteronomy 5:6-21

80 Romans 7:25

81 Matthew 5:3

feeling fortunate. To be "at the end of your rope" means you are experiencing hopelessness and helplessness.

Jesus's audience included the physically ill, the emotionally disturbed, and those oppressed by **demons**. These are the same kinds of people who seek help in our counseling rooms. Let me ask you: How can Jesus call "the poor in spirit"—those people who are so distraught emotionally that they are begging for help—"blessed"? According to Jesus, the spiritually distraught arrive at a place of well-being only when they are "at the end of their rope." Why? Because in that position, they crave more of God. When I am close to feeling desperate and giving up, I know that I pursue the presence of God more intensely.

What does Jesus suggest we do to help the seeker who admits to spiritual impoverishment? We, givers, are to comfort these people. In the next verse, Jesus says: **"Blessed are those who mourn, for they will be comforted."**[82] Comforting people who are at the end of their rope is one goal in both psychotherapy and faith-based counseling. To mourn is the same verb as "to lament" or "to wail." Is this not the picture of seekers in deep depression? Shouldn't we, as givers, join them in their grief?

How do we bless and comfort the heartbroken? The heavenly Father gives us His Holy Spirit, that facet of God who comes alongside to encourage us. Jesus described the Holy Spirit as the Comforter or Helper, and said, "…the Advocate, the Holy Spirit, whom the Father will send in my name, will teach you all things…."[83]

Over the years, I have found that secular "talk therapy" is not as effective as I would wish. So for me, the **role of the Holy Spirit** becomes critical in therapy. Why? Because the Holy Spirit is both the Creator *and* the Comforter. In both roles, He knows the soothing love language unique to the person, is privy to all the things assaulting that wounded soul, and has intimate knowledge

---

82 Matthew 5:4

83 John 14:26

of His child's inner traumas. Once these are identified, the Holy Spirit is present to heal and comfort him.

Please note: When we counselors rely on "secular principles" to treat depression, we do not have this godly advantage because we are not operating from God's divine perspective and revelatory knowledge. At times, I have failed to partner with the Holy Spirit and have found my success rate of getting at the problem's root cause to be mediocre at best. However, when I rely on the Holy Spirit, praying and seeking His wisdom and words of knowledge, discovery is well over 80 percent. I believe when clinicians use the gift of the Holy Spirit, their patients will heal and start to function in life more quickly.

Be Humble (Meek) Before God...and Be Blessed!

In the Beatitudes, a third tenet focuses on a person's need to humble himself before God, which is noted in this beatitude: **"Blessed are the meek, for they will inherit the earth."**[84] Meekness is a mindset of humility. The "meek" person relinquishes his self-interest and follows God's choices. He is trusting in God's goodness and allowing God to take control.

Not all, but many, secular clinicians suggest that their clients do *not* surrender to a higher power. (A well-known exception to this is Alcoholics Anonymous [AA]; AA members are encouraged to admit that they need to rely on a Higher Power.) Rational humanists encourage their patients to move into self-reliance and independence, not into surrender and dependence on God. So, why would Jesus have suggested something so radical as to be humble? What is the health benefit of turning your life over to God?

When you become a meek one, the Bible says you inherit the earth! In other words, when one has an attitude of dependence on God, the heavenly Father gives you a spiritual bank account

---

84 Matthew 5:5

from which to draw. You inherit God's riches, and that helps to restore you to a fruitful and productive purpose.

This principle highlights a conflict between secular and faith-based thinking: Should a person be self-reliant or God-reliant? Perhaps the Creator suggested that we be God-reliant because when someone has an attitude of independence (i.e., self-reliance), it leads that person to greater frustration and grief.

I believe dependence on God reduces one's anxiety and establishes his inner peace. But this approach is a paradox. When we release ourselves to God, we may see that the path He is taking us on is barren and rocky, one strewn with danger and pain. Why would anyone want to walk into a wilderness landscape? Psychologist Dan Allender pointed this out: In moments of crisis, a human being seeks help from either God or some little god, which includes one's independent self. Wilderness walking encourages me to partner with the Mighty God, not the puny god that I am or the object I've grabbed onto for help. Allender reflects on this paradox: "Why would God have us walk through danger to get to Him?...Because the danger draws us to a greater dependence on the only One who can provide and protect."[85]

Stop Working to Be Perfect...and Be Blessed!

If you have a perfectionistic drive, you will be interested in this fourth principle: **"Blessed are those who hunger and thirst for righteousness, for they will be filled (satisfied)."**[86] Striving to achieve perfection is stressful. All counselors recommend that clients stop running after perfection. Yet, there is an innate desire in us to be perfect. The perfectionists with whom I work must have all their ducks in a row and be flawless all the time. Perfectionists struggle with feeling dissatisfied in most situations

---

85 Dan B. Allender, *The Healing Path: How the Hurts in Your Past Can Lead You to a More Abundant Life* (New York: Random House, 1999), 21.

86 Matthew 5:6

and say they don't see themselves as "good enough." They never feel in control because they are going after perfection, which is an impossible goal to achieve. What an exhausting way to live! I encourage them to let go of that worldview.

When we have this perspective (i.e., "I must do this perfectly"), we strive to achieve perfection in our own power. Yet, God's definition of perfection is different from ours. According to God, to be perfect is to have faith that Jesus's righteousness has made us right in God's eyes. God sees us as perfect; this is a spiritual condition, not a state of goal completion. True perfection can only be achieved through Jesus and His death on the cross.[87]

When we change our worldview and pursue the goal of being right in God's eyes and not in our own human perspective, God gives us divine satisfaction. There, we no longer need to strive for perfection. As we hunger for God's righteousness, He satisfies us. Then, we can relax into contentment and accept our human condition of imperfection as a temporary state, corrected when we enter heaven, knowing God sees us as perfect right now because of His Son Jesus.

Ask the Spirit to Clean Out Your Heart...and Be Blessed!

Further along in the Sermon on the Mount, Jesus suggests another solution to stress, the fifth beatitude. Jesus says, **"Blessed are the pure in heart, for they will see God."**[88] What does "pure in heart" mean? The word "pure" is defined as free from contaminants or inappropriate substances. A cardiologist can show us, physically speaking, whether one has a "pure heart" by doing an angiogram. If there is any blockage, the doctor can correct it by placing a stent in the artery. However, in the emotional heart of a person, we cannot place a stent if there were

---

87 Galatians 3:2-3

88 Matthew 5:8

to be a blockage. We can, however, talk about releasing one's toxic emotions of bitterness and resentment.

For people working with mental health issues, an important treatment goal is reducing the seeker's stress. Just like the cardiologist, we givers need to assess the condition of the person's heart. In therapy, the question is: **Which emotions, housed in the heart, might be causing an unhealthy blockage?** Some of these questions can arrive at answers during "talk therapy," but not all.

Man's wisdom is limited. Yet, we can ask the Holy Spirit to reveal the problem and to recreate healthy blood flow, spiritually speaking. Let's consider God as the Divine Cardiologist; He knows what is going on within a person's heart. When one turns his heart over to God, the Holy Spirit cleans out the junk and changes the negative emotions to healthy ones.

Once we have pure hearts, then what does God do for us? This verse promises that we will *see* (or experience) Him. Would not one's staying focused on Jesus be the final solution to mental illness? Surely, God calls us to fix our eyes upon Jesus, and then we will not grow weary and lose heart.[89]

Become Workers for Peace...and Be Blessed!

As the last beatitude, Jesus suggested we become peacemakers: **"God blesses those who work for peace, for they will be called the children of God."**[90] Lack of peace is the biggest stressor in the world at large (wars!) and within our own tiny sphere of life (discord!). Finding peace is the goal of those who have emotional problems. If givers were to pursue only one emotion for seekers to master, it should be peace. Anybody who struggles with anxiety and irritability wants peace. Anybody whose mind is swamped with negative and toxic thoughts wants

---

89 Hebrews 12:2-3

90 Matthew 5:9, New Living Translation

peace. Any family who faces domestic violence wants peace. The fact is that we all want *shalom,* the Hebrew word for peace. It means completeness and soundness in body and soul. Shalom peace is the *antidote* to being "out of control." This spiritual resource comes into our lives when we let the heavenly Father handle everything, freeing us from chaos and giving us safety and security.

Jesus, who is the Prince of Peace, tells us He came because of our needing peace.[91] The Bible declares, "...the punishment that brought us peace [*shalom*] was on him [Jesus], and by his wounds we are healed."[92] This beatitude challenges us about the value of *shalom* and the importance of this truth: When we work on behalf of Jesus, His peace blesses us and returns us to mental well-being.

Love Your Enemy...and Be Blessed!

When Jesus finished preaching the "Beatitudes," His Sermon on the Mount continued, covering other topics. Jesus introduced this idea: "Love your enemies," even while He knew this attitude was radical and life-changing. How often do we givers and seekers talk about the "enemies" in a person's life? How much therapy time is used venting about those who bully us, criticize us, and give us a hard time? Consider this: If you forgave your enemy, do you think you would *feel* differently?

Jesus challenged us even further when He warned us not to lose our temper. He said if we lash out and call someone a "fool," we are subject to judgment. Doesn't this standard seem unattainable? Then Jesus declared something impossible, "Be perfect, therefore, as your heavenly Father is perfect."[93]

---

91 John 16:33

92 Isaiah 53:5

93 Matthew 5:48

How can we achieve perfection? We can't! Not in our own power. We just read that we become perfect because of our connecting with God. The heavenly Father sees us as perfect through our imputed (i.e., assigned) righteousness from Jesus. Once connected, God gives us the power through the indwelling Holy Spirit to do things we normally can't do. In Jesus, we have the ability to love our enemies, to manage our anger, and to handle criticism and persecution. "Loving your enemy" does not come from a stony heart but from a Holy Spirit download. Jesus is right there to forgive us and clean us up. Then He gives us what it takes to forgive.

Remember the symptoms of someone with a mental illness? They include negative *emotions* such as irritability, sadness, shame, and guilt, to name a few. Also, the *behaviors* of someone with mental illness include impairment in relationships, immoral choices, fits of rage, selfish preoccupations, drunkenness, and frantic efforts to avoid loneliness. When the seeker has surrendered to the Holy Spirit, he is set free from these problems and is motivated to stop the acts of the sinful nature and to demonstrate spiritual fruits (i.e., godly traits) such as love, joy, peace, and patience.[94]

The Importance of Forgiveness

In this same sermon where Jesus talks about our being perfect, He also challenges us to forgive. Part of loving our enemy is forgiving him. How many of us struggle to forgive someone who has wronged us? The foundation of many emotional problems is the root of unforgiveness. Therefore, we need to look at what Jesus said about forgiveness.

Why should we forgive? First, we forgive because we ourselves would like to be forgiven. Second, God expects us to

---

94 Galatians 5:19-26

forgive *if we want God to forgive us*. "...Forgive them, so that your Father in heaven may forgive you your sins."[95]

The fact is that holding on to unforgiveness corrupts the body and the soul. And yet, in our human strength, to forgive someone who has wronged us seems impossible. We need the faith of God and the power of the Holy Spirit to do that heavy-duty forgiving.

In Rodney Hogue's book on this subject, he illustrates forgiveness like this: When I hold a person responsible for a wrong done to me, I am holding him on my emotional hook of unforgiveness. Even though God has asked me to forgive him, I may not *want* to forgive him for several reasons. For one, I don't want to remember what he did. So I'll deny the experience of wrongdoing and avoid having to make the choice to forgive. A second reason may be that I'm angry and want to seek revenge. A third explanation might be this: If I forgive him, I am conveying the message that what the person did to me was "ok."

Our seekers, particularly those who have experienced abuse, neglect, and trauma, need to wrestle with this question: Have they forgiven their perpetrator? To forgive is a **choice**; it is not a feeling. When one recognizes the need to forgive and chooses to forgive, the Holy Spirit will help. All one has to do is ask the Holy Spirit to take the offender off the personal hook and place that person on God's hook. Now God becomes the one "revenging," and the emotional load of the offense shifts off the seeker and onto the shoulders of Jesus.[96]

Take One Day at a Time...and Be Blessed!

Because emotional issues load a person down, the Lord suggested we live one day at a time. The weight of multiple problems can feel unbearable. Life is just too much for many

---

95 Mark 11:25

96 Rodney Hogue, *Forgiveness* (Instantpublisher.com, 2008).

people. Perhaps that is why the Lord suggested this simple idea: Live one day at a time. For me, this suggests that, at any given time, I put one portion of trouble on my plate and take only small bites of that problem. While I "eat," I thank Jesus that He is taking responsibility for the rest.

This philosophy—to live one day at a time—is echoed in therapy offices, AA meetings, and church pulpits. Living one day at a time is a completely different approach to life than the characteristic hustle of our western world. If we'd manage a single problem one day at a time, we would be more at peace. With this strategy, we'd release to God control of details, including the dimension of time. We'd see things from Father God's point of view.

The Bible tells the story of Moses leading God's people out of captivity in Egypt toward the Promise Land. God gave them food to eat, only one portion each day.[97] Why did He do that? To emphasize their daily dependence on God as the heavenly Father. Choosing to trust God the Provider every 24 hours for our needs takes the emotional load off us.

This kingdom principle is so important that it's one of the first suggestions I share with my clients. "Please," I say, "just take one day at a time. Scripture says, '…and as your days, so shall your strength be.'"[98] Jesus urges us not to worry about tomorrow because each day has enough trouble of its own. Before He made this suggestion, He gave us a command followed by a promise: "But seek first his kingdom and his righteousness, and all these things will be given to you as well."[99]

---

97 Exodus 16:12-26

98 Deuteronomy 33:25, English Standard Version

99 Matthew 6:33

PART THREE:

EXPLORING THE LANDSCAPE OF FAITH

8
FACING TOUGH QUESTIONS AND SPIRITUAL CHALLENGES

E ARLIER WE ESTABLISHED that faith can benefit healing, but "having faith" is not that simple, as my clients have pointed out. Seekers talk about the tough questions with which they grapple, and the wrestling match goes well beyond the question of "Does God exist?" It goes to the mat of tough questions like, "Will God *really* love me?" or "How can I understand the suffering I face?"

In Chapter 5, I proposed ways to introduce the topic of faith into sessions. The next step is to give the seekers freedom to investigate questions with you, at which time you operate as their guide, not the problem-solver. They ask the questions, and you listen, remembering that they must arrive at their own answers. Hopefully the seeker will be a person who respects the Scripture. Opening the Bible to key places that shed light on the questions may be all you are called to do.

Can I Believe in God?—The Question of Unbelief

When people experience emotional distress, wounded seekers often say it is difficult to believe in God. They may have tried praying their way out of pain, and the god they were praying to didn't answer. Or, they had believed their god would not permit emotional pain. But when he did, they declared, "I just don't believe in God. If there were a god, he wouldn't let me go through all this." A frequent statement is this: "I've tried God, but it didn't do any good." Soul pain has a way of eroding the foundation of any faith and potentially destroying it.

Based on my half-century of experience, people who have a humanistic (i.e., non-God-centered) worldview have harder times overcoming mental illness than people who have faith. Conversely, people who believe in a personal God have a greater success rate handling mental health problems than those who don't have faith. God has given people freedom of choice. Many people choose to use rational humanism as the cornerstone of their worldview. This philosophy excludes powerful ingredients that could manage soul pain; several attitudes that help are unconditional love, a purpose in life, and a hope for the future.

Sometimes, if a person's heart is restless, I simply ask if he would like to consider the option of resting in God. This question opens up the topic of the very existence of God. Obviously, I can't prove the existence of God, but I share one of two classic responses if the seeker says, "I can't believe in God."

First, Augustine of Hippo, a saint in the Catholic Church in 300 A.D., wrote this oft-quoted sentence: "Thou hast made us for thyself, O Lord, and our heart is restless until it finds its rest in thee."[100] If the seekers identify profound restlessness within, I suggest they consider "trying God."

Second, I suggest using Blaise Pascal's wager on this very topic. Pascal was a 17th century French Catholic theologian who wrote:

> Belief is a wise wager. Granted that Faith cannot be proved, what harm will come to you if you gamble on its truth and it proves false? If you gain, you gain all; if you lose, you lose nothing. Wager then without hesitation that He [God] does exist.[101]

---

100 "Daily Archives: August 28, 2014," Catholicism Pure Simple, accessed June 05, 2019,

http://www.catholicismpure.wordpress.com/2014/08/28.

101 "Pascal's Wager," Wikipedia, April 20, 2019, accessed June 05, 2019,

https://en.wikipedia.org/wiki/Pascal's_Wager.

To put it another way: If God does not exist, and you wager that He does, *and* you live as though He does, then during your life, you will be content. And, in the end, if it turns out that God's existence is false, you have lost nothing. If, on the other hand, you wager that God does not exist, and thus live as though there were no God, *but* you discover at the end there is a God, then you have a *big problem*.

My father made a similar wager.

At my age of 27, my Dad's 58-year-old twin suddenly died of a heart attack. My father's father (whom I never met) had died at that same age for the same reason. There I was, loving my 58-year-old father and wondering what was going to happen to him for eternity.

We had this conversation:

"Dad, I know you're a good man, a rational, scientific thinker. Until now, you have said that you don't believe in God. But, frankly, I'm scared for you. Uncle Oliver just died. He was your twin! Your father died at the same age. And I don't want you to die, unsaved, and fail to go to heaven. So could we talk about this?"

We sat in his home on a cold January day in 1973, sipping hot mulled cider.

"Julie, you know I'm a man who needs proof. I need to see and feel and touch something to believe it." He picked up his mug and rotated it as though he were looking for answers. "I have to admit the life you have lived since you became religious has piqued my interest in God. You claim He has changed your life. You certainly think He's real. But I simply can't believe that."

"Ok, Dad. I get it. But would you try something for me? Could you pray a prayer something like this...."

I suggested a prayer he could pray as an invitation to Jesus. I reviewed how the Creator showed Himself to us through the incarnation of God in Jesus. I went on to explain that Jesus's death on the cross had the purpose of making us right with God. And I concluded by stating that

Jesus had been resurrected from the dead. All Dad had to do to be saved was make a commitment to Jesus.

"Daddy, the whole point is for us to know Him personally, through the Holy Spirit," I said.

"I'll tell you what, Julie, I'll pray this...." And my kind-hearted, skeptical, analytical father prayed: "God, Julie says You exist. If that is true, I need to see proof. So based on her faith in You, I ask You to show me the truth about You. Do You exist? Can I trust You? Amen."

Three months later, Daddy and I attended an Easter service during which the pastor preached a message about the proofs of the resurrection.[102] Dad left that service and said, "I get it. What do I need to do now?" He went home and prayed with me to receive Jesus into his heart. He did the symbolic act of pounding a worthless wooden stake into the garden just to lay claim to his newfound faith. From that point forward, we had terrific times sharing about Jesus.

One year later, I visited him again on Easter. At the end of that weekend, Daddy and I prayed, after which he handed me a bouquet of daffodils and forsythia and said "goodbye." That was the last time I saw him. Three weeks later, he died suddenly of a heart attack at the age of 59. He was calling on the name of Jesus as he suffered the fatal cardiac arrest.

My father's death was the saddest experience I had up to that point in my life. During the decade before his death, I had wrestled with some fundamental questions about the character of this God in whom I had come to believe. These concerns came rushing to the forefront of my thoughts because of this heartbreaking loss. If it were God who "let" my father die so young, where was His love in my experience?

---

102 Brent Landau, "The Case for Christ: What's the Evidence for the Resurrection?" The

Conversation, August 31, 2018, accessed June 05, 2019, http://theconversation.com/the-case-for-

christ-whats-the-evidence-for-the-resurrection-75530.

If There Is a Good God, Why Do Bad Things Happen?—The Question of God's Character

During high school I struggled with this question—Why do bad things happen if there is a good God? Many explanations weigh in on this, but fundamentally, it is an **unanswered mystery**. When a person is stumbling through life with inner pain and "bad things" are going on, he flounders when his faith is under assault. When he can't answer this question, he gets stuck; his growing faith may even stop developing. My mind searched and debated. Where is God's goodness in difficult times?

As a high school senior, I didn't have trouble believing God existed. My intellectual furnace had been stoked by the Interfaith Club speakers. However, I received no helpful answers about *God's love for me*. Where I got stuck was in believing God is good *and* that He loves me. Therein lies my challenge! How did I know, how could I trust, that God really loved me?

Two months before high school graduation, I heard an evangelist tell me why Jesus died. On April 17, 1964, the Spirit of God shook my heart and mind with the love of God. I *knew* that God loved me. Why? Because this perfect man, Jesus, chose to lay down on a wooden cross to die—for me. Jesus allowed the Roman soldier to take a spike and hammer it into His hands and feet—for me. God's Son was tortured for three hours and took upon Himself all the sins of the world—for me! In that moment, I realized God died for me personally, that He forgave my sins, and that He loved me unto death. I there and then committed my life to Jesus, and a powerful peace came upon me. Because of it, I no longer needed to have *all* the answers. I opened my heart and surrendered everything. I was transformed from the inside out and found my *place* in Jesus's love.

Since then, the answer to the profound question of how a good God can allow bad things to happen has taken me a lifetime to ponder. While the best answer to **how can God be loving and**

still allow suffering in this world remains "it's a mystery," there are key points to consider.[103]

"Because of our free choice" is one answer to the question. God—in His love for us—gave us the choice to love Him or not. When Adam and Eve chose to question God's Word, they decided to disobey Him. With that choice, evil entered the world right at that moment. Why? Because the minute human beings succumbed to the temptation of the serpent, the devil became the prince of the world.[104]

This **reality of evil** points to three other considerations when thinking about "bad things happening." First, we have a spiritual enemy, the devil. While we live on this earth, we are in Satan's domain of darkness. Originating from this realm are death, disease, and decay of our bodies, souls, spirits, and society.

Second, God's grace and His merciful goodness have softened the blow of evil and have buffered the influence of the enemy. Jesus's death destroyed the power of evil and Satan.[105] However, we will see the full results only at the End Times.

Third, we live out our earthly existence on **this side of the veil**. Kevin L. Zadai, who had a near-death experience and found himself on "the other side of the veil," wrote, "The membrane between the spirit realm and the physical realm is but a thin veil."[106] We humans have our feet planted in the domain of evil where "bad things" do happen, while God and the angels are working on the other side of the veil to accomplish divine purposes. God is constantly working all aspects of our lives

---

103 Julie Caton, "Why Do Bad Things Happen to Good People?" Drjuliecaton.com, December 22,

2017, http://www.drjuliecaton.com/why-do-bad-things-happen-to-good-people.

104 John 16:11

105 John 12:31; John 14:30

106 Kevin L. Zadai and Sid Roth, *The Agenda of Angels* (Shippensburg: Destiny Image Publishers,

2019), 65.

together in a manner that enriches us spiritually.[107] Yes, we may suffer. However, God's love meets us in that suffering.

Mental health issues are connected to our suffering (either causing it or resulting from it), so I will address a psychology of suffering at the end of this book. In the meantime, let's continue to explore the mystery of mental illness.

Is There an Enemy of Our Souls?—The Question of Darkness

When soul pain or mental illness overwhelms people, they often feel they are under some kind of attack. People have said to me, "I don't know what came over me." Or, "This anger (or hopelessness or fear) was so much more powerful than I am." Or, "These feelings (or thoughts) are bizarre; I don't feel like myself anymore." Because of these comments and others like them, I began to wonder if this domain of darkness, in which evil resides, had some hidden agenda. Could it be that an enemy with a purpose, intelligence, and a will is attacking our souls?

My life experiences pushed me deeper into more questions such as these:

- What is the best solution for helping people?
- Why was I struggling within my soul even with Jesus in my life?
- What was causing my husband's lack of respect for me?

Because of my own issues, my understanding of the soul was not helping me cope well. I needed to learn more about the spiritual part of me.

I hungered for the Word of God, particularly the sections about Jesus giving us His Spirit. Jesus said:

---

107 Romans 8:28

123

If you ask me anything in my name, I will do it....The Father will give you another Helper, the Spirit of Truth, and we will make our home within you. The Holy Spirit will teach you all things and you will bear fruit that will remain.[108]

I wanted harmony in my marriage and greater compassion as a therapist. I yearned to connect with this Spirit of God and to see the Holy Spirit overcome the darkness in this world.

After we were married, Rex and I moved around for eight years while I supported him as he finished his education. Then we settled near his parents, and Rex and his father bought a dairy herd. We had a son (1978) and a daughter (1980). During my first pregnancy, I helped with farm chores and returned to school for a Master's degree in counseling. At first, Rex was opposed to that decision, but I pointed out that getting a higher education would increase my earning capacity, something necessary because we were in dire straits financially due to the depressed dairy industry.

Needing God's Spirit in the Face of Loss

On January 17, 1982, our lives changed abruptly. Before dawn, Rex and I went to milk the small herd of 60 cows. The outdoor thermometer read 0°F, with a -40°F wind chill blowing. We discovered that all the water pipes and the vacuum pump (a machine necessary to milk the cows) were frozen.

While Rex set up localized heaters, I milked, a two-hour chore. This was my first time running the milking machines. Usually, I just cleaned the udders. Then, we walked the 600 yards over crusted, icy ground back to our house. I happened to look over my shoulder and was stunned to find the barn roof and loft ablaze in flames!

Our fight against the barn fire began. Volunteer firemen arrived, and while firemen sprayed water, it froze in mid-air. Rex, encrusted with ice, ran into the burning barn over and over again

---

108 Adapted from John 14 and 15

to unclip the cows standing in their stanchions and shooed them out. Firemen escorted the cows through icy conditions to a neighbor's barn. Sadly, some young stock and a few horses died in the barn fire. The next day we sold the dairy herd for reduced prices in a "stress sale," causing us to lose a great deal of money. Now, Rex and his father were without employment.

During this period, I had been working part-time as a social worker at a small private agency. The barn fire shook my faith. How were we going to have an income? But God faithfully provided for us. A few days after our loss, the county mental health clinic offered me a full-time job with benefits as a psychotherapist. Because of the loss of our meager income, I accepted the offer. However, taking the job was against Rex's wishes, as he wanted me to stay home part-time with our children, ages two and four.

Five years later, I was still employed with the community mental health clinic. By God's grace, the University of Buffalo's Ph.D. program in psychology recruited me. To complete this degree, I worked as a therapist four days a week and used vacation time to meet the academic requirements of field placements. Classes were held in the evenings. I finally graduated in 1994 and returned full-time as a psychologist to the mental health clinic. All told, I worked there off and on for 16 years in various roles. Throughout that time, with my supervisor's permission, I used strategies to incorporate faith into my psychotherapy sessions. I was then, and continue to be, a firm believer that forming a healthy identity was key to stabilizing one's psychiatric problems. And there is no better way to find one's identity than for a person to surrender to Jesus, His Creator, and to become a **Christ-one** (Christian).

Needing God's Spirit in the Face of Persecution

During my Ph.D. internship in a large city hospital in 1990, I faced one of the most challenging years of my life. About a month into the internship, the chief of the Psychology Department asked us interns (the two young men and me) to stay late to review a testing protocol.

After-hour meetings had not been discussed as part of our job requirements, so I was a bit confused. I said, "I'm sorry, sir, but I have clients at home. I can't stay." (During the evenings, I had been seeing clients in private practice for Christian counseling.)

"What!?" he said, leaping out of his chair. Glaring at me, he said, "You have clients elsewhere?"

"Yes, I've had a Christian counseling practice for a few years," I said, the blood rising into my neck and cheeks.

"You absolutely cannot do that," he shouted. "First, you are a student *here*. Until you get your license, you are not to provide counseling services. Second, what do you mean 'Christian counseling?' Are you a fool? Haven't you read the diagnostic manual? It says that a 'strong religious belief' is classified as a **mental disorder**."

The large, bristle-haired professor circled the conference table, coming toward me. He slapped his hand on the books in front of me. They bounced. He shouted, "You *will* stay for my meeting. Cancel those patients. You *will* see me later to discuss stopping this, this…'Christian practice' immediately."

My heart beat like a hummingbird's. My stomach rolled. I blinked away my tears. Then I steeled myself, prayed, and prepared to meet with this supervisor to shut my practice down. (It had been providing us a meager income.)

Later that day, when I entered his office, I felt like a bug about to be stomped on. The supervisor scrutinized me. "So you are a Christian? Well, let me tell you this—that is a myth," he sputtered. "It is worthless. Believing like that weakens people. By the time you leave this program next spring, you will have ceased such foolishness. Now, tell me about these 'Christian' clients of yours. You and I are going to discuss their discharge from your care right now."

With that, I experienced a year that stressed me to the max. All nine members of the psychology department would describe themselves as "rational humanists scientists" who wanted nothing do to with religion or faith. While I was oppressed repeatedly for my beliefs, I privately clung to the Spirit of Jesus. Throughout that year, the staff supervised me with mortifying intensity, finally placing me on probation. With one month to go in the academic year, they said they would not certify my internship unless I stayed for another year.

I made one of the hardest decisions in my life. I quit. I could not trust them. But I prayed, "God, if you want me to be a psychologist, there has to be another internship. I know You will see this through."

Despite the injuries to my pride and my growing distrust of people in my profession, I had learned a lot. God knew what He was doing. The prosecutorial atmosphere at the internship drove me deep into prayer. I grew in my reliance on Jesus's Spirit. Two years later, God provided another internship, this time at a children's residential treatment facility. By 1994, I was a licensed psychologist with a broad array of skills working at the local mental health clinic. Within four years, I left the clinic and established a full-time private practice as a Christian psychologist. Soon, my business was thriving with referrals from pastors, doctors, and lawyers. Rex, who was unemployed at the time, became my office manager.

9
THE HOLY SPIRIT
UP CLOSE AND PERSONAL

Breaking Down Denial

A S I START my seventh decade, I am reviewing the difficulties of my personal life. I still struggle with soul pain, wounds of the heart, and ungodly misperceptions. But God has blessed me with personal encounters with the Holy Spirit and has increased my understanding of what true wholeness is. Jesus's philosophy and techniques have been the pivot point for the work I do. My personal relationship with Christ anchored me while I was in the midst of a difficult marriage. As time went by, I still felt something spiritual was missing. I was close to Jesus. My faith was growing. And Bible study and prayer sustained me—but I craved a deeper relationship with God.

During the time our children grew from toddlers to young adults at the farm, my husband would release me from my responsibilities (as wife and mother) on Sunday afternoons while he watched football. In those few hours, I enjoyed riding my Palomino mare Miel. The beautiful, blonde quarter horse would canter across the alfalfa field, and I swayed in rhythm on her back, the wind rushing against my face. This ritual ride was the one moment every week when I felt free to connect with the Creator in a special way—just my horse, my God, and myself, surrounded by nature.

After an exhilarating run on Miel, she and I would slow down as I would let her rhythmic walk clear away my mental congestion. You would think that after achieving a doctorate in psychology and creating a successful practice that I would be able to thrive emotionally. But I could not.

The rest of a typical week went like this: I spent hours treating clients in my home office and helping with chores. Rex, who had been working for two decades in a variety of jobs, acquired a Master's degree in social work and worked as a clinician. While I felt fruitful in my private practice, the rest of my life was an emotional wasteland because the quality of my marriage had deteriorated.

Even though Rex earned his bread and butter as a social worker, he refused to go with me to couple's therapy. Nor would he allow me to seek counseling myself, and at first I honored his request. I felt like a deflated helium balloon, wanting to fly but tethered to a bowling ball, unable to be myself.

By 2003, I realized that my husband had neither respected me nor accepted me for who I was for many years. And I did not have the courage to speak up. But, one day, the proverbial cat got out of the bag, when Rex and I were RV traveling in Canada. We had parked at a marina and had gone to a tourist kiosk to retrieve and pay for a week's worth of emails. (Those were the days!) A week earlier, I had emailed my sister about my heartbroken feelings regarding my marriage. To this email, she responded and acknowledged her own sadness about my marital difficulties.

Rex and I opened that email together. It was the evening before my 57th birthday. At the moment I clicked "open," Rex, standing behind me, read my confession to my sister: "For the last 25 years, I have felt neither respected nor accepted for who I am." Fear of Rex's anger washed over me like molten lava, and my stomach sank. Rex turned on his heel, seething, and walked away.

He did not return that night to the parked RV and stayed away a total of 18 hours. When I saw him next, on the afternoon of my birthday, his anger was still palpable. His only response was: "We have gotten through other tough times, so we will get through this." Yet, nothing changed. He didn't bring the topic up again, nor did he change his behavior—and really, neither did I, so flummoxed by his anger and reticence.

On a spiritual level, I felt stifled and unable to operate as the Lord prompted me. My husband insisted that he knew God's will for my life and directed me accordingly. The church culture around me said I was under the marital obligation to obey my husband in *all* things. On an emotional level, my heart was breaking because any ideas and inspiration I had were quickly squashed by Rex. I felt imprisoned in my own home and saw no way out.

For 25 years, I had been living and working in the home we had built. I now earned sufficient money as a counselor. Habitually, Rex and I had morning coffee and briefly studied the Bible together. Year by year, we rotated through various churches, each one chosen by Rex. Despite these facts, I might as well have wrapped my heart in bandages and put a strip of duct tape across my mouth, because I felt no freedom to be myself.

One outlet available to me was a monthly meeting with a small group of Christian women. These three ladies believed God meted out different kinds of suffering. As I shared my marital heartache with them, one said. "Of course, you need to stay with him. It's the suffering God has put on your plate. You can vent to me any time. But you can't leave him. Divorce is out of the question." I agreed—marriage was until "death do us part." I prayed to know and to do God's will.

But by 2005, more issues came to a head. For one reason, my daughter, who had recently graduated with a Master's degree in social work and had been married for two years, was visiting our home from out of state. During that Christmas week, she observed her parents' marriage for the first time in a decade.

One morning she came to me sobbing. Expressing her concern, she said, "Do you realize, Mom, that you are a classic picture of an emotionally abused wife?"

Her words cracked into and hammered down my wall of denial. Patterns of communication in our family weren't healthy—I knew that. But I, a psychologist, would not have called the situation "abusive." I had been raised by a critical, controlling mother. I had been educated to put my husband first. I had been taught the biblical mandate of silence and submission. So, this emotional environment was the "norm" and the right way of doing things. Wasn't it?

My daughter was right, but I was not ready yet to take full ownership of that truth. I prayed to understand how to bring positive change, but denial blocked me for another six months. My husband continued to refuse permission for me to enter therapy for myself, saying all I needed was the Holy Spirit to be my counselor. At my wit's end, I started seeing a Christian counselor without Rex's permission. Sadly, I felt a heavy load of guilt for "disobeying." On the third session, when she called my husband a "dumbass," I quit going.

Breaking My Bones

Another change was the loss of my beloved horse, Miel. At the age of 30, the Palomino had become so decrepit from arthritis that we euthanized her. But I yearned to keep riding, so I went to "try out" another horse that was for sale. Because Rex had been objecting to the purchase, I went without my husband's knowledge. The horse owner observed me while I rode the horse around the inside ring in the barn and then out into the pasture.

The next thing I knew, an ambulance was rushing me to the hospital while I cried hysterically and faded in and out of consciousness. The horse had stumbled in a hole, throwing me forward and off. My wrist took the full weight of my fall and looked like a corkscrew, a distorted S-shape, grotesque appendage. When my husband met me in the emergency room, he was livid with anger. "How dare you venture out to try a horse without my permission," he said. "If I had been with you, this never would have happened."

Doctors treated me for three broken ribs, a serious concussion, fractured teeth, as well as a spiral fracture of the right wrist. After the wrist surgery was performed, the orthopedic surgeon said, "It is one of the worst wrist breaks I've seen. I've done the best I could." With a metal plate and cadaver bones in my wrist, I returned home with a twisted right arm and a thumb locked in place alongside the index finger. Even so, I was grateful for the extent of the healing because I was still able to type and to write, to hold my coffee mug, and to pull clients' charts out of the filing cabinet.

Perhaps this accident emboldened me. Perhaps experiencing the dreadful, physical pain strengthened my "I-can-handle-anything" muscle. Perhaps it made me aware of how short our lives can be. For whatever reason, our marital communication changed. I started to speak up, always respectfully. I declared my right to discern God's will for my own life. I stated my point of view. Rex became more and more angry with my new boldness. When I disagreed with him, I would say, "Oh, I hear you. You think I should do it *that* way. Well, I disagree with you. From my point of view, I believe doing it *this* way is better."

This approach created friction. He would throw a plate across the room, kick a hole in the wall, or fling a lamp, shattering it. His response to my stated opinions was either increased aggressiveness or a passive sullenness during which he would not speak to me for days.

I pleaded with him (again) to go with me for therapy, but he said things like, "I am not going to let anybody else peek under your hood." Or, "I don't need a counselor; I have the Holy Spirit."

In October 2010, Rex acted out dangerously, and I heard the Holy Spirit say, "You are no longer safe. Now is the time to go." Let me add two important details. First, when that happened, I had not yet developed much of an ability to hear the Holy Spirit. I had not been taught it was an option. So I have to thank the Lord for speaking so clearly that His voice broke through my untrained ear.

Second, just days before this incident, several friends had separately reflected their concerns for my safety and sanity. One of them offered me a safe house. So, when the Spirit commanded me to leave, I vacated my marital residence and took my precious belongings (anything that my husband might smash or destroy) to the safe house. I rented space in a nearby church to keep my business going, and within six weeks, I was safely relocated to my new home. My clinical practice continued to thrive, and I was grateful for God's provision and protection. But my heart was broken. My right wrist, although "healed," remained twisted and somewhat immobile—perhaps a symbolic statement of my soul.

The Spirit Quickens Me

At this point, the two roads I had been trudging down changed course. The mental health road, where I had been a practitioner for four decades, took on a different landscape. Now, I became the patient. Also, the landscape for my spiritual life changed. I was no longer on my husband's road where he was doing all the "driving." Now, liberated from his control, I could read the Word of God and **pray in the Holy Spirit** as long as I wanted, the way I wanted. I could move **as the Spirit led me**.

I found freedom in both experiences. My new therapist, Laura, was sensitive to my faith position even though she was a secular counselor. Her techniques cleared away the debris of denial about my abusive marriage. She comforted me when I expressed feelings of devastation for having failed the marriage, and she introduced me to stress-relieving techniques that brought deep healing.

I started attending a different church, one that respected both my gender and my gifting. I was not shunned for being divorced. For the first time in my life, I heard that Jesus heals today just as He did 2,000 years ago.[109] I saw people experience physical healing and other **outpourings of the Holy Spirit.**

Two years later, I was in a bike accident and broke my left wrist and elbow, also dislocating my right middle finger. The orthopedic surgeon braced and bound my finger, and cast my left wrist and elbow on a Monday. The next day, while I was trying to function as normally as I could as a therapist, I received a call for the first time from a representative of an international Christian ministry that I had been supporting for two years. After he introduced himself, silently I groaned, assuming he called to solicit donations. I was sore, tired, and frustrated, and didn't want to deal with him. But he said, "We just want you to know that the Holy Spirit prompted us to call and pray for you this morning. What is it that you need?"

I broke down in tears and told him what had happened. Over the phone, he asked the heavenly Father to provide divine healing and to meet other important needs. By Friday, I was without any pain, and all of my needs were cared for. One week after the accident, the doctor re-x-rayed me and declared me healed. "A miracle," he said.

Three years later, a team of five women, whose goal was to minister to females who were homeless, destitute, victims of human trafficking, or recently released from prison, asked me to join them as a speaker. With this team (Thirsty Ministry, Inc.), I attended Cultivate Revival with Randy Clark in October 2015. I was beginning to feel that God was redeeming my shattered life.

Before I continue, let me share Keri Cardinale's testimony. She is the musician on the Thirsty team. We are dedicated to introducing the love of Jesus into women's lives. Each of us has had life-changing encounters with Jesus.

---

109 F.F. Bosworth, *Christ the Healer: Sermons on Divine Healing* (Grand Rapids: Baker Books, 2000).

While some of the people who have shared testimonies in this book understandably have chosen anonymity, Keri has signed her name because she is confident that God is using her story to minister to many other people through her musical talents and life-coaching skills.

Keri Cardinale's Testimony: Redeemed From a Lifestyle

When I was 15 years old, I fell in love with Jesus. I met Him in the basement of an old Catholic Church. He was my everything. I would sit in my classroom and daydream about Jesus. It felt good to be accepted and loved. I wanted to be the best Christian girl out there.

Then I met a boy. My first boyfriend! How exciting! Someone liked me—that chubby girl who had her prom dress especially made because she couldn't fit into any of the dresses at the mall. My life took a turn when we slept together and I had sex for the first time. The night I gave away my virginity was like the morning I gave the key to my soul to a psychic. All I wanted was to "be known."

Yet, this decision sent me down a path of believing God would never forgive me for what I did. I lost trust in men and God...and then ran into the arms of my best girl friend in high school. At the time, I believed I loved this girl; she accepted me exactly the way I was.

With this choice, I entered into a life of homosexuality for 15 years. The more I accepted this as my life, the more I spiraled into a deeper and darker world. I ended up heavily involved in the occult, studied to be a psychic, praised the gods of the universe, dabbled in the underground club world, and saw things I wish I never saw.

But while I was busy being my own god, I was secretly searching for the God I once knew when I was a child. In June

2007, I stood at a crossroads. I was faced with the choice to accept my current girlfriend's marriage proposal or to walk away. I felt trapped. Walking away meant giving up everything I had known to be true in my life. I was torn. I called out to God for help. Little did I know, the uneasiness I felt was God's voice drawing me back to Him. I decided to walk away from the life I was living and to trust in something bigger than myself.

That day, I stood in the presence of Jesus with my heavy, over-packed bags of luggage. Jesus looked me in the eye and said, "Choose Me, Keri." Instantly, I felt this unexplainable love and dropped my baggage. I chose Him. This was the most intimate moment I have ever experienced. It was the moment that I was "made known" by the God who created me.

This is the love I have always longed for. Jesus picked me up, cleaned me off, renewed my mind, and re-wired my desires. My biggest desire in life was to "be known." Now that I am fully known by God, there is no turning back.

Keri Cardinale, www.kericardinale.com

[Watch for Keri's book *Swing Wide*, to be released by Bridge Logos, Fall 2019.]

The Spirit Heats Up My Life

On the evening of October 22, 2015, I heard Randy Clark speak for the first time. The event was my maiden voyage to a "faith healing" conference. Until this point, I had not heard of Randy Clark, nor anything about **words of knowledge** or "**going down in the Spirit.**" So, when Randy said, "The Lord gave me the word that someone in this audience [of 1,500 people] has sustained a spiral fracture of her right wrist," I was shocked. That was so specific! But I had come to the conference with great anticipation. The miracle in 2012 had taught me to expect the supernatural! I got out my iPhone and took a photo of my crippled wrist.

That night my life changed, again! I went forward, and a first-year student at the **Global Awakening School of Supernatural Ministry** asked me a few questions about the wrist and the accident. She wrapped her hand around my right wrist and prayed for the Holy Spirit to come. I felt heat enter my fingers, wrist, and arm. As the heat increased, the bone in my wrist melted like clay. She prayed for 30 minutes, and my wrist bone continued to straighten. The frozen thumb was able to move across my palm, from the index finger to the middle finger. I was at least 85 percent healed. The love of God poured over me in a way I had never experienced before. I **collapsed in the Spirit** and wept.

Because of that miraculous healing, I studied online with Global Awakening's Christian Healing Certification Program (CHCP). Since January 2016, I have studied physical healing, deliverance, and inner healing. My learning curve has been progressive and steep. The Lord has given me the privilege of participating in diverse divine healings. I have seen miracles happen in the bodies and hearts of people. I even witnessed the **casting out of a demon** of fear oppressing a patient, whom I had been treating with paranoia for five years.

In December 2016, I traveled with the Global Awakening team to Brazil, during which time I had the opportunity to discuss this book's outline with Dr. Randy Clark. One of the participants at that **revival** in Ponta Grossa was a 35-year-old wheelchair-bound lady named Rafyhna. Crippled at birth due to oxygen deprivation, she had never walked. With members of the Global team praying for her over three days, Rafyhna was freed from spirits of depression and suicide. This courageous lady moved her legs, planted her bare feet firmly on the floor (for the first time ever), and walked![110] We were thrilled! My memory of Rafyhna moving her legs, as the Holy Spirit poured through her, still takes my breath away. Gratitude floods me. I have been in touch with

---

110 Doreen Morehouse, "Global Awakening Brazil - December 2016," YouTube, December 23, 2016, accessed May 22, 2019, https://www.youtube.com/watch?v=T1xS39XM_QI&t=202s.

Rafyhna via emails and video calls. She is facing new battles (some emotionally), but she is growing stronger physically, mentally, and spiritually.

There is thrill in the victory of a healing, but there is also agony in the defeats we see around us.[111] Rafyhna's story is one example of why we must do away with the disharmony and suspiciousness between the mental health and faith communities. These groups need to learn from each other, to live in harmony, and to embrace the full repertoire of our callings. The freedom we can see in Rafyhna's life illustrates what God can do when we all work as one team.

Let's share our toolboxes!

---

111 Randy Clark, *The Thrill of Victory/The Agony of Defeat* (Mechanicsburg: Apostolic Network of Global Awakening, 2009).

10

TRANSFORMATIVE BELIEFS: UNDERSTANDING HOW CHRISTIAN DOCTRINE HELPS THE CLIENT

To BE EFFECTIVE, any giver needs to have a basic understanding of theology because the seeker may arrive interested in connecting with God. When givers are operating from a faith-based position, they should be capable of exploring the seeker's belief system. Sound Christian doctrine is foundational because one may discover that a seeker's problem is based on misunderstanding Scripture. This error needs to be corrected in order to bring full healing. If the givers start with a secular model, they need to know who this Christian God is and what benefits Jesus offers seekers. When the givers reflect an understanding of the seeker's faith language, it enhances the healing process.

Two primary doctrines impacting mental illness are as follows: the powerful event of **the crucifixion of Jesus** and the subsequent **downpour of the Holy Spirit at Pentecost**. Here is further explanation.

Christians have faith in one God.[112] The **Trinity of Christianity** is described here by the Apostle John: "For there are three that bear record in heaven, the Father, the Word [Jesus], and the Holy Ghost: and these three are one."[113] This religious doctrine of the Holy Trinity is the cornerstone that empowers the

---

112 Deuteronomy 6:4

113 1 John 5:7, King James Version

followers of Jesus. That single doctrine contains the dynamic ideas that make believing in Jesus Christ so life-changing.

The **Lord Almighty is the heavenly Father**, the Most High God, and our Perfect Creator. Because of His perfection and condition of holiness, sinful people cannot enter His Presence. Because we are corrupted by sin, God's holiness would destroy us. We "sinners" need an advocate, mediator, or deliverer; all of these roles are carried out by Jesus.

Jesus bridges the gap between sinful man and Holy God. Jesus, whom God conceived in the womb of the Virgin Mary, became the Son of Man, whose purpose is several-fold: to model God on earth, to die a sacrificial death, to erase sin, and to defeat the evil one. Jesus's death was followed by His resurrection from the dead. This historical event unleashed **God's power source, the Holy Spirit**, who connects man with God in a personal relationship. In short, **Jesus is God-made-flesh**.

When God came to earth as Jesus, His role was to be our Savior to seek and to save the lost.[114] The "lost" are people like you and me who could be ruining our lives and setting ourselves up for destruction (i.e., eternity in hell). God invites people to bring their imperfections before Jesus, to admit they deserve a punishment for their sins, and to embrace Jesus's death as that penalty. In that process, they are made righteous through Christ. Once made righteous because of Jesus, each person can enter the presence of the Holy God.[115] All of this happens by God's grace.

The Holy Trinity is a complex topic that I will oversimplify with an apt metaphor. In this metaphor, God—who is the all-powerful, all-seeing, ever-present Creator of the universe[116]—is equivalent to the substance we know as water, H_2O. The Creator/Father God wanted to reveal Himself to mankind. To do

---

114 Luke 19:10

115 Hebrews 9

116 Genesis 1:1

so, He had to present Himself in tangible, visible form. As a result, the Christ child was born,[117] which is called the Incarnation. Jesus grew up to become a carpenter from Nazareth and stepped into His ministry to bring the kingdom of God onto earth. So, while the Father God is the liquid H_2O, Jesus is the equivalent to ice, a solid form of H_2O, easily seen, touched, and handled.

The Father and the Son wanted to share their divine energy with mankind, so they unleashed **the Holy Spirit**. The downpour of the Spirit of God came 50 days after Jesus was crucified, buried, and resurrected. The Spirit came as a violent wind into a room where many followers of Jesus were praying, and enabled the believers to speak in unknown languages and to preach boldly. In my metaphor, the Holy Spirit is the steam form of H_2O, the same substance as God the Father and Jesus the Son, but experienced by a human being in various ways, such as warm mist or a moist breeze.[118] If a person does not make the choice to have the Spirit of Christ in his life, he simply does not belong to God.[119]

When people struggle with emotional problems or mental illness, they need two fundamental solutions: something to crush the root of the problem and then a source of empowerment to reestablish a healthy life. These **two primary doctrines—Jesus's death/resurrection and the outpouring of the Holy Spirit— accomplish this uprooting and transforming.**

Do You Believe in a Personal God?

Faith-based counselors love to tell their stories to secular workers and their patients. In varying forms, this is what we say: "There is a God, *and* I have experienced Him." This is a fact that I would die for. It is so important that I want to ask every

---

117 Luke 1:31, 35

118 Acts 2:1-4

119 Romans 8:9,16

skeptical giver this question: "Do you believe in God, particularly a personal God?"

If you are reading this book, I propose that at some level you do have belief in "God" and are concerned about suffering. You see the dichotomy between health and sickness. You recognize the existence of good and evil. You may have experienced "emptiness" in your own soul, suggesting that you sense the condition of spiritual "fullness." You may have felt "imperfect," which means you embrace the abstract of "perfection." Each of these inner experiences stems from one's innate sense that there is a God. Whenever you are yearning for health, goodness, fullness, and perfection, this craving in your soul emerges from that part of your brain wired for God. Your need confirms that you know in your heart of hearts that there is a God.

The Judeo-Christian belief in God is that the Creator is a loving Person who created man in His own image. God is a thinking, feeling, willful, living being, and we are just like Him (without His divinity of course). This God, Jehovah, the Existing One, wants to have a relationship with us. He created us to be God's glory. Sadly, we succumbed to pride in the Garden of Eden and disconnected ourselves from God.[120]

Partnering With God Repairs One's Brokenness

Here is God's solution to our brokenness: When God created man and woman, He saw them as good, good people.[121] For an undetermined season, Adam and Eve enjoyed the heavenly Father's presence in the Garden of Eden. They frolicked naked and experienced no shame or guilt. They lived for the purpose God gave them: to enjoy His presence, to cultivate the Garden, and to bear fruit. The Lord God gave only one command, "You are free to eat from any tree in the garden; but you must not eat

---

120 Romans 3:23

121 Genesis 1:31

from the tree of the knowledge of good and evil, for when you eat from it, you will certainly die."[122]

Despite what God said, Eve tuned her ear to another voice. She listened to the enemy of God, who was masquerading in paradise as a serpent. The crafty devil said to her, "Did God really say you couldn't eat of that tree? Oh, come on, Eve. If you eat of that fruit, you won't die. You'll become like God."

That sounded good to Eve. (Don't we all want to become like God?) She took the apple, ate it, handed it to her husband, and he ate it. With their actions, they said, "We would rather eat the apple and be like God than to obey God. We want our independence." (Don't we find ourselves saying something like: "I can be independent and handle life on my own"?) With that prideful act of disobedience, mankind fell into sin and severed our connection with God. Overcome by fear, Adam and Eve pulled away from God and hid, just as some of us do.

Even while His heart was broken, Father God still loved us. He designed a plan for our rescue and repair. When Adam and Eve disobeyed, shame and guilt overcame them, and they grabbed fig leaves to cover their nakedness.[123] But God knew this fig leaf solution would not work in the long run, so the Almighty made garments of animal skins and clothed His children with them. (This is the origin of the biblical expression: "…without the shedding of blood there is no forgiveness."[124])

Because of man's independent self-will, God cursed the man and the woman. God also cursed the serpent[125] and said to the devil something along the lines of: "I will put conflict between you (and your minions) and the woman (and her human ancestors). In the end, her Offspring (i.e., Jesus) will crush your

---

122 Genesis 2:16-17

123 Genesis 3:7, 10

124 Hebrews 9:22

125 Genesis 3:14-19

head (i.e., the devil)." This was the beginning of all **spiritual warfare**: good battling evil.

God the Father planned that God the Son would become the "animal skin" for us in our sinful state. Throughout the Old Testament, the sins of a Jewish person could be forgiven when a spotless lamb was sacrificed on the altar. Thousands upon thousands of lambs had their jugular veins cut by the temple priests in Jerusalem for this purpose. Each lamb's death took the punishment for a Jewish person's sin. Then biblical history moved ahead thousands of years, and the cross of Christianity came into the story. Jesus was the final lamb slaughtered for the sins of mankind.

This event, the crucifixion of God, is the key to my becoming a Christian. I surrendered to God because I was convicted of this fact: My Creator loved me so much that He willingly died by crucifixion in order to pay my "fine' for being a sinner. Jesus was the Lamb that I allowed God to slaughter for my sins. When I acknowledged that act of love and received Christ as my Savior, my life changed.

Why did my life change? Because **the Holy Spirit entered me** at the time of my repentance. I became a new person through God's generative power, the divine energy flowing through me.

The Holy Spirit is the Person of the Trinity who repairs the brokenness in our relationships. Let's consider in more depth who the Holy Spirit is. The Holy Spirit is God, and as such, He has a personality. The Spirit has thoughts, emotions, and a will. He is God's means of direct communication with our minds. The entire Trinity, all being Triune God, has the greatest power in all of God's creation. On one end of the spectrum, the power of the Holy Spirit sustains the universe, and on the other end, He—the spiritual form of our personal God—is directly accessible to us through prayer. By invitation, the Holy Spirit does curl up in your heart.

(If having the Spirit of God in you sounds appealing, all you have to do is acknowledge Him. Just say, "I repent of my sins. I need Jesus. Holy Spirit, please come in to me. Thank You." And He will.)

Let me ask you this important question again: *Do you believe in God?* Many people say they believe in something "out there," some force "bigger than themselves," a "higher power." Right now, I am honing in on that question and am asking:

Do you believe in a personal God, one who loves you and wants to change your life?

If your answer is "no," I'm sad for you because you are missing out on experiencing divine love. In addition, you face the serious problem of living without God for eternity. But I challenge you to an experiment because this is such an important decision: to believe or not to believe in our Father in heaven.

Try this experiment: Suspend your disbelief for one month. What do you have to lose?

Say this prayer:

"I don't really believe in You, God. I have my reasons. But my life is not going very well. So, for one month, I'm going to ask for a gift of faith: Your faith, not mine. Based on what I'm reading, I ask You to reveal Yourself to me. Meet me where I am. Speak to me in a way I will understand. I have nothing to lose by this gamble and everything to gain. Thank You."

If your answer is, "Yes, I believe in God," then this book is going to be an eye-opener. You are now in a position to have the Holy Spirit download new ideas to you. You can learn more ways to help people who struggle with mental illness. The Holy Spirit is the Author of the Bible. Many people complain that they can't understand what they read in Scripture. I suggest that they ask the Author of the book to sit beside them and actively explain points as they go along. The Author will make the book come alive. The Holy Spirit will lead you into a deeper walk with God. This growth will enhance your own mental health. As you serve others, you will glow with joy and peace.

Do You Believe That God Will Be Good to You?

If you are a reader who said, "Yes, I believe in a personal God," then here is my next question:

Do you believe God is good and loves you? Do you think God desires what is best for you?

Many people find that question harder to affirm. If you believe God is a good, good God, take a second—right now—to thank Him for His goodness.

But, if you are having trouble believing in God's goodness, let me make two suggestions. First, reflect on whether or not you have projected negative characteristics onto God. Perhaps in your childhood you experienced punishment, abuse, or neglect, and you have projected this emotional reality onto God. Ask God to remove these misperceptions. Recall Randy Clark's testimony where he admitted he projected his perception of his father ("one-who-does-not-always-show-up") onto Father God. Through awareness and prayer, Randy was able to change that misperception.

Second, check out what kind of faith you are using. Perhaps you are not using the right kind of faith. Maybe you are using your limited *human* faith. Expand your concept of faith for a moment. Jesus said in Mark 11:22, **"Have the faith of God."** I am suggesting you believe with the same type of faith that our Creator has.

What type of faith does God have? Look at the first words in the Bible:

> In the beginning God created the heavens and the earth. Now the earth was formless and empty, darkness was over the surface of the deep, and the Spirit of God was hovering over the waters. And God said, 'Let there be light,' and there was light.[126]

---

126 Genesis 1:1-3

148

This is the kind of faith God has. The Almighty God saw the emptiness, the nothingness, a huge, dark void. And He did something. He breathed His energy into that emptiness; He created light and life. That is what the faith of God is all about. Consider this:

- ❖ The **faith of God** calls into existence that which does not exist.

- ❖ The **faith of God** brings health out of sickness, light out of darkness, joy out of sadness, sanity out of craziness, and life out of decay.

- ❖ The **faith of God** sees chaos and brings peace. God faces a raging sea and commands the turmoil to cease. God sees our hatred for our enemies and fills us with the capacity to forgive. God rebukes death and regenerates us with resurrection power.

Is this the faith you want to have? If so, simply ask for it. Faith and the Spirit are both gifts from God, and He gives without measure.[127]

The faith of God in me has helped my own emotional healing process and has benefitted my clients, no matter what their ages or stages of development are.

---

127 John 3:34; Ephesians 2:8

11

THE CROSSROADS WHERE PSYCHOLOGY MEETS JESUS: AN APPLICATION OF ERIKSON'S PSYCHOSOCIAL STAGES OF DEVELOPMENT

MOST TRAINED CLINICIANS **use a developmental template** to conceptualize their clients' mental health problems. Using such a construct can be helpful in the same way a GPS can navigate a trip. There are different theories of personality development, and they have one thing in common: They look at the influence of the seeker's early environment on his personality development. I selected Erik H. Erikson's **Psychosocial Stages of Development** because his theory includes all three facets of the human being: the body, soul, and spirit. The ultimate goal of counseling is to encourage the seeker to be stable emotionally, to think soundly, and to relate well to others. When people succeed in each of Erikson's stages, they have acquired good mental health.

In the following, I describe the intersection of these two roads—Erik Erikson's Psychosocial Stages of Development and the Person of Jesus. Bringing these two together best illustrates how the faith of God—when activated by Jesus—can form a healthy personality.

I discovered Erikson's framework while working on my Bachelor's degree thesis on the Negro Slave Personality. My research on how slaves emotionally and spiritually survived captivity brought me to Erikson's theory of identity formation. Based on ex-slave memoirs and Negro spirituals, evidence pointed out that the healthy choice for the enslaved person was to form his identity by having a relationship with Jesus Christ. Thirty-five years later, research for my doctoral dissertation had the same findings: Identity formation was the primary stabilizing factor in the psyche of someone diagnosed with Borderline Personality Disorder. Today, as the first step in overcoming emotional issues, I encourage my seekers to strengthen their sense of identity.

My respect for Erikson has lasted a lifetime. Of all the psychologists I've read, Erikson demonstrates sensitivity to the spiritual nature of man. In his personality analysis of the Reformation's Martin Luther, Erikson wrote: "Religion elaborates on what feels profoundly true even though it is not demonstrable; it translates into significant words...the exceeding darkness which surrounds man's existence."[128]

Erik H. Erikson (1902-1994)[129] left for America in 1934 just as Hitler took over his country, Germany. Several psychosocial factors influenced his thinking: his illegitimate birth and subsequent problems with personal identity; his affiliation with Sigmund Freud's daughter, Anna, and her psychoanalytic thinking; and his German-Danish Jewish upbringing.[130] Erikson's work highlights the personality traits of trust and identity, and freedom from shame and guilt. He weaves them throughout his developmental stages.

In 1953, as a professor at Harvard University, Erikson introduced the important concept of "identity formation" and coined the term "identity crisis." Consolidating one's identity is

---

128 Erik H. Erikson, *Young Man Luther: A Study in Psychoanalysis and History* (New York: W.W. Norton & Co., 1962).

129 Erik H. Erikson, *Childhood and Society* (New York: W.W. Norton and Co., 1950); Erik H. Erikson and Stephen Schlein, *A Way of Looking at Things: Selected Papers from 1930-1980* (New York: W.W. Norton and Co., 1987).

130 Lawrence J. Friedman, *Identity's Architect: A Biography of Erik H. Erikson* (New York: Scribner, 1999).

the key to maintaining a stable personality. My doctoral research concluded this: When a troubled patient—one with a long history of emotional problems, fear of abandonment, and interpersonal chaos—forms a strong identity, it becomes an anchor to help stabilize her dysfunctional behavior. Furthermore, my research showed that a person achieves a sound identity and gains freedom from her emotional issues[131] when she enters into a personal relationship with Jesus.

To illustrate how psychological theory intersects with the Christian faith, I describe Erikson's eight stages of psychosocial development, and how the grace of Jesus brings a positive resolution to the emotional challenges a human being faces.

Stage One:
Basic Trust vs. Mistrust—God Alone Is Trustworthy

Stage One focuses on the child's healthy trait of having a sense of basic trust. This trust is formed when the baby receives consistent love and nurturance during his first few years of life. If the child fails to develop trust, he will grow up to be plagued by attitudes of suspiciousness and anxiety. When Jesus is introduced to someone who is distrusting and fretful, three important things happen. First, the person, by turning to Jesus for help, can confess his lack of trust, suspicious feelings, and anxious thoughts. Then, Jesus forgives and cleanses the person. Finally, **the Holy Spirit replaces the seeker's unhealthy traits with those of trust and love.** These steps transform the person so he can say: "I'm a beloved child of the heavenly Father."[132]

---

131 Julie B. Caton, *An Application of Erik H. Erikson's Psychosocial Theory to the Borderline Personality Disorder* (Submitted to the Faculty of University of New York at Buffalo in partial fulfillment of the requirements for the degree of Doctor of Philosophy, June 1993).

132 John 1:12

Stage Two:
Autonomy vs. Shame and Doubt—Jesus Took the Shame

The positive trait in Stage Two is that of autonomy, where the two-year-old child has discovered his own mastery of toilet training, walking, and talking. Sadly, if the child is subject to unhealthy responses from his parents, he may slink off into the closet with overwhelming feelings of shame and doubt. Shame, a toxic trait, is both an emotion as well as a thought.

So how does the life-changing Spirit of Jesus benefit the adult carrying a load of shame and doubt? **Jesus promises a relationship that does away with shame.** A scriptural promise is: "[The Lord declares] 'Do not be afraid; you will not be put to shame. Do not fear disgrace; you will not be humiliated.'"[133] Paul the Apostle wrote, "Anyone who believes in [Jesus] will never be put to shame."[134]

What makes Jesus the antidote for our shame? There are two factors: First, Jesus modeled managing shame. His life events, particularly His illegitimate birth, the arrest, torture, and crucifixion, targeted Him with shameful assaults. He moved through them with grace. Second, the Bible says a divine exchange took place. When He gasped His last breath and gave up His spirit, Jesus *took our shame onto Himself.* In so doing, He removed the cloak of shame from us and thereby *set us free.* When a seeker encounters the crucified Christ, and says, "Thank you for dying for me," he experiences a profound liberation from shame and doubt.

---

133 Isaiah 54:4

134 Romans 10:11

Stage Three:
Initiative vs. Guilt—Jesus Settles the Problem of Guilt

Erikson's Stage Three evolves around the tension between initiative and guilt. The school-age child can get stuck between taking creative action or standing passively by while people reject his initiative. His guilt is a nagging and toxic emotion, an unpleasant feeling that he has done something wrong. But **Jesus's death overcomes one's guilt**.

There are **two types of guilt**—true guilt and false guilt. "**True guilt**" happens when our consciences kick in and confront us with something we've done wrong. We feel true guilt when we have broken a law, acted contrary to a cultural expectation, or disobeyed our "god." (Here, "god" is whatever or whomever we use for our final measurement of acceptance in life.) The Christian experiences true guilt when he recognizes he has fallen short of God's absolute standard, causing him to feel disconnected from God. But God, wanting us to be connected to Him, has a plan to free us from true guilt. We become free when we ask for forgiveness through the shed blood of Jesus.

Or we may experience "**false guilt**," a toxic emotion resulting from the judgment (actual or perceived) of others, ourselves included. This counterfeit guilt stems from our fear of losing that person's respect.

In addition to having true guilt when we disobey a law, or having false guilt when we internalize the judgment of someone, we also can experience guilt because of accusations from an evil spirit. The Bible uses the name "Satan" to label the evil one, which means "the accuser."[135] False guilt, Satan's primary tool to derail us emotionally, is nothing more than guilty feelings being rooted in the lies of the accuser. The prophet Isaiah wrote: "What

---

135 Job 1:6, New Living Translation

sorrow for those who drag their sins behind them with ropes made of lies...."[136]

Here's **the solution when you experience guilt**: If you have true guilt, confess your wrongdoing, and ask for God's forgiveness in the name of Jesus. If need be, go to the person you offended and ask his forgiveness. If you have false guilt, put the opinion of others, self, and Satan in perspective. Simply identify the lies, repudiate them, and turn them over to Jesus, thus disempowering the enemy of your soul (Satan).

The following is a testimony from a retired schoolteacher who experienced true guilt. Let her tell you what God did.

LJ's Testimony: Freedom From Guilt

As I write this, I am well into my sixth decade. I look back now at my twenties and thirties and thank God that He intervened in my life. He loved me so much that He relentlessly pursued me and saved me from the brink of destruction.

According to modern society, homosexuality is not a sin. It is no longer a stigma practiced in secret. Lesbians have "come out" of the closet, and their shame has been removed. If you believe otherwise, they tell you that you are politically incorrect.

When I fell into that alternative lifestyle as a young adult, I felt this way. Over a period of 19 years, I had two female partners. It started rather innocently with my college roommate. For 10 years, I was in a relationship that was much more about companionship than sex. Then I was lured away by an older woman who was experienced in sexual pleasures. When lust got a hold of me, it took me down a long and dirty road.

---

136 Isaiah 5:18, New Living Translation

During the last few years of that relationship, the Holy Spirit worked on me. I realized what I was doing was not pleasing to God. Up to this point, I had not been worshipping Jesus, but now I felt a pull toward a local church. More importantly, I began reading the Word of God. What a powerful influence the Bible had on me! The Holy Spirit took a hold of me and shook me! Portions of Scripture made it perfectly clear to me that homosexuality is an abomination to God. (See Romans 1:21-27, also 1 Corinthians 6:9-10.) Our body is a temple of the Holy Spirit, who lives in us. We are not our own. We were bought at a price. Therefore, we are to honor God with our body (1 Corinthians 6:18-20).

I "came out." I came out of homosexuality. Many people say it can't be done, but they can't argue with me because I have done it. When I left homosexuality behind, I'm pretty sure there was a party in heaven. It is no longer just a choice between homosexuality or heterosexuality.

The choice is this: Do I obey God and His Word, or not?

Don't get me wrong. I didn't do all the work. The Holy Spirit worked in me. The Word of God was medicine for a broken life, a soothing salve for a sin-sick soul, and the Word, who is Jesus, started the healing that was so long desired.

LJ, 65-year-old retired teacher

Stage Four: Industry vs. Inferiority—God-Confidence Is the Antidote

Industry vs. inferiority, the task school-age children face, is seen in this psychological dilemma: Should I work hard and be industrious, or succumb to feelings of "I'm less than the others"? If a child has successfully achieved Erikson's first three stages, he usually does not feel inferior. For this reason, working on this psychosocial task does not often happen in the counseling room because most of my clients have problems rooted in mistrust, shame, and guilt. But if he does struggle with inferiority, he can take initiative and **develop self-confidence through a relationship with the Creator.** Jesus replaces the person's sense of inferiority with God-confidence.

Stage Five:
Identity vs. Role Confusion—Identity as an Anchor

To achieve good mental health, one's identity is the most critical characteristic a person needs. Identity is the sustaining nature of who a person is, no matter what else is going on. Erikson called this important stage "Identity vs. Role Confusion."[137] Identity, the tool that prepares one for adulthood, is the anchor with which a person uses to stabilize himself, no matter the storms swirling around him. Identity becomes his stable harbor throughout the rest of his life.

If and when Jesus is introduced into one's therapy, the seeker has the option of entering a personal relationship with Him. If the seeker so chooses, **Jesus provides a God-given identity** in two ways: First, the Son of Man can become the person's life example. Jesus's lifestyle and philosophy can become a platform for the directionless client. Second, when the person surrenders to Jesus, the Holy Spirit transforms his heart, anchoring[138] it by providing hope, trust, and love.

Stage Six:
Intimacy vs. Isolation—Surrendering to God Supports Intimacy

Healthy intimacy is the next task: "Intimacy vs. Isolation." Here, the definition of intimacy means a close, personal

---

137 Erik H. Erikson, "Psychological Issues," *Identity and The Life Cycle: Selected Papers* 1, no. 1

(New York: International Universities Press, 1959), 101.

138 Hebrews 6:19

relationship, and <u>does not imply an act of love-making</u>. Once young people establish their identities, they want to fuse themselves with another person. This drive toward intimacy is particularly "hot" in young adulthood because of the biological urge to procreate.

In order to "lose oneself" in another person, young people need courage. A firm sense of self overcomes fear and helps the process of entering into a close relationship. Leif Hetland restates the word "intimacy" to sound like *"into-me-see,"* and says it is "a process of opening yourself up to be seen."[139] This deep connection with another person is what God desires—not only for a man and a woman in marriage—but for a believer to really know God Himself.

Mental illness can negatively affect one's interpersonal relationships. Often, the stress of an intimate bonding is too much, and people—who can't face the challenge of intimacy—have emotional crises. People may be afraid of exposure and getting too close. Or, they may be so hungry for connection that they overreact and devour the other person. Either response—withholding (out of fear) or possessiveness (out of neediness)—ends in heartache. The fear of intimacy fades when one has surrendered to God first. Why? Because the **born-again relationship becomes the safety net** under the tightrope of intimacy. Jesus helps reduce the fear of personal closeness and creates a healthy balance.

The key to navigating this stage is asking God to be the first Person with whom you are going to be intimate. Jesus suggested these are our priorities: "Love the Lord your God with all your heart and with all your soul and with all your mind....Love your neighbor as yourself."[140] When we reverse this divine plan and love ourselves above others, or love others above God, we put God last on this priority list. Consequently, unhealthy emotions

---

139 Leif Hetland, *Called to Reign* (New York: Convergence Press, 2017), 143.

140 Matthew 22:37-39

arise, such as anxiety and guilt. Having **Jesus orchestrate this stage of intimacy clears the way to healthy relationships**.

Stage Seven:
Generativity vs. Stagnation—Having God's Spirit as the Source of Generativity

When adults achieve this seventh stage, people are in the season of being "empty nesters." Hopefully, these middle-agers have raised their children, found their niche in life, become productive and creative, and exuded psychological health. They are experiencing "generativity."

However, if their life's purpose no longer exists, these people then feel a profound stagnation, and seek help. Erikson wrote, "Mature man needs to be needed."[141] Often when adults have emotional problems, they no longer feel needed. They think they're incapable of generating anything of value. Their mood worsens. So, when they **partner with the Creator**, the Person who designed them with a purpose, this newfound meaning in life creates **a sense of generativity,** and puts an end to their stagnation.

Let me share a story about Kendra, a school speech therapist and mother of two athletic, school-age boys. She came to me because of the onset of panic attacks. She had a heart's desire to help all children but was being derailed by anxiety and depression. Because she carried the baggage of sexual abuse trauma, Kendra had a perfectionistic mindset and needed to be in control. Her job was demanding, and she had to put up with a critical boss. Then, tragedy hit: The mother of one of her boy's teammates went missing for a week and was found murdered in their village. This triggered Kendra's anxiety.

---

141 Erikson, *Childhood and Society*, 267.

Kendra's Testimony: Jesus's Spirit Restored My Inner Life

When I thought of that mother murdered, dead and gone, and her boy never seeing her again, it was just too much. I began to panic at random times, probably when I didn't have control over stuff. When I drove my car, my anxiety was triggered. Being called into my supervisor's office for a lecture became intolerable. Managing all the details of our family's busy life made me crazy.

But in counseling conversations, I realized the rituals of my Catholic religion had never given me inner peace, something I desperately wanted. My parents had not taught me how to have a relationship with Jesus. I'm grateful that my therapist asked me about my faith and kindled a connection with Jesus. Now I see the difference between religion—which is what I had—and a relationship, which is what I've got now. Jesus is showing up everywhere!

I'm finally learning how to partner with Jesus—to call upon Him for peace, to ask Him to control the uncontrollable, and to free me from the fear of dying and never seeing my boys again. Today, I can talk on the phone with friends, and I don't go into a downhill slide emotionally. When people start to complain about this or that, I am able to shift toward the positive and let go of the negative. I can stand back and see how God has been actively transforming my life to get me to this point. My life's dream is to create a business to help children. Now I can see God working, and I am feeling peace while He brings this dream into reality.

Kendra, age 45, speech therapist and mother

Before her panic attacks kicked in, Kendra's life might have been described as "stagnant." She was going through the day's activities, checking off her to-do lists, and doing her duty to job and family. However, her apathy found her sinking deeper into a joyless existence. Through the process of counseling, she discovered how a vital relationship with Jesus could lift her out of that stagnant life.

Jesus is an excellent solution to "stagnation," a problem that often rears its ugly head in therapy. In recent years I've been a speaker at many women's retreats, facilitating discussions. At these events on psychological wellness, the participants frequently complain: "I don't feel I have a purpose anymore." Or, "Every day is the same; it's just ho-hum-ho-hum." When I ask these people how they spend their time, they admit they're not invested in any productive outlet. They read their Bibles, do their chores, play on their computers, help a shut-in occasionally, and go to church on Sundays—but they feel blah and stagnant. Life seems meaningless.

When the spiritual stagnation within people disappears, their emotional symptoms go away as well. Do you know how a once-healthy pond becomes stagnant? Water still runs into it, but something has happened to block it from running out. So algae slimes around the edges, and decaying leaves and plant life muck up the pond. The water has no place to go. In a similar manner, a person can become stagnant and fouled-up. The people may be filled with God's love, but if they are not releasing that love, they, too, can become like the lifeless pond.

God has much to say about getting rid of stagnation and living a revitalized life. Some people say that their lives are flat and depressing, despite their relationship with Jesus, but they are paying little attention to the Holy Spirit. They are unaware that the Holy Spirit wants to do exciting things through them. Or perhaps they don't believe they are good enough to have an empowered partnership with God. So God (and I) urges them to re-examine their relationship with the Holy Spirit.

When Jesus ministered on earth, on a daily basis, He and His disciples shared the Good News, fed the hungry, clothed the poor, healed the sick, and cast out demons. (Jesus *and* the disciples even resurrected the dead!) When we encourage one another to invest in these aspects of Christian ministry, we break up the stagnation in our lives. When we give of ourselves and serve, we become like a beautiful, clear, freshwater pond through which vital water will flow, causing the generation of new life.

A sure way to live a life of generativity is to participate in a **revival**. I have had the privilege of traveling with Global Awakening teams on mission trips. People in South America, Africa, and India are hungry for the Holy Spirit. Revivals are common there. We see people experiencing *salvation, impartation, healing,* and *deliverance*. In the West, there are more revivals now than a half century ago. M. James Jordan says, "a true revival is when God's presence shows up with extreme power. It is an overwhelming release of His presence in a particular place."[142] Interested? Just pray this prayer:

Holy Spirit, break up my stagnant waters. Flow into and out of me, using me like Jesus. Under Your power and by Your hand, I want to preach, heal, and deliver. (And, yes Lord, I want to resurrect the dead, too!)
In Jesus's name, Amen.

Let me introduce Darla, a youth pastor I met on a Global Awakening trip to Brazil. How she loved to dance with the children during worship! As a spirit-filled Christian, she had a passion to pour her energy into ministering to young people. She decided, in order to be more effective with the teens, that she needed to know what counseling referral sources were available. In the process, she ended up receiving inner healing.

Darla's Testimony:
The Holy Spirit Regenerated Me

*My journey with inner healing began 15 years ago when I was introduced to **theophostic** prayer. As a youth worker, I*

---

142 James M. Jordan, *Sonship: A Journey Into Father's Heart* (Taupo, New Zealand: Fatherheart Media, 2014), 20.

desired to learn more so I could assist the teens during their emotional journeys.

__Theophostic__ praying, or __sozo__ therapy, is based on the Greek word meaning "complete healing of body, soul, and spirit." This method, new to me and completely different from traditional counseling, included Jesus in the process. Before I suggested it to the teens, I became a counselee. At the time, I did not realize I needed inner healing, but I soon learned that early childhood experiences had negatively shaped my emotions and caused me inner pain.

During my therapy, a situation came up from my childhood that I had previously labeled "a game." That word choice was my desperate attempt as a child to mask the damage of an act of molestation done to me. The pain and scarring had been so extensive that, during the __theophostic__ session, I could not even speak of it and became catatonic. Finally, someone helped me write out what had happened, and I was able to put voice to the memory.

As part of the sozo process, Jesus was invited into the pain of my experience. My Lord showed me where He had been during that time and the truth about my circumstances. This devastating incident had never even come up in previous "regular" therapy. I had repressed it deeply. But the Holy Spirit revealed it.

During the pain of Spirit-driven recognition, I realized I had been a victim in that situation. Because I had an understanding of Christ's love covering me, I now was able to face the wound. I processed my emotions and gained freedom from the pain. The Holy Spirit comforted me through it.

My coworkers and family will tell you of the changes in my life. Prior to receiving this inner healing, I was emotionally erratic and often pessimistic. My diagnosis was probably "depressed" or "cyclothymic" (i.e., mood swings). Now, I am even-tempered and optimistic.

Since this time, I have worked with many women to address their emotional issues and past wounds. All of them had tried to avoid going back into that place of pain and shame. But once they felt loved and safe, they accepted the challenge to dig into the wounded areas of their lives. Through the introduction of Christ and the Holy Spirit into their pain, they healed.

Why? The Holy Spirit offered them something to fill the empty holes left by their evicted pain. Healing is a process. Often, emotions get worse before they get better. But when the person embraces this stage of suffering, continues to work through the pain, and affirms herself through the love of Jesus, she receives complete healing. I'm grateful I've seen this in myself and in many others.

Darla, youth minister

Stage Eight:
Ego Integrity vs. Despair—Accepting Your Own Life Cycle

In his psychosocial developmental template, Erikson's final stage focuses on "Ego Integrity vs. Despair." By this time in life, when people are working on this last task, they have accepted the triumphs and disappointments during their walk on earth. They feel that they have fulfilled life's purpose and are at peace with their own choices. They face the reality of upcoming death without fear. These psychosocial traits indicate that the person has achieved ego integrity.

Sadly, people who are aging often find that their emotional wounds have festered. They have become embittered and feel anxious about anticipated suffering and upcoming death. They mask their worry through a tough exterior of control. They are unable to forgive their own errors and are left in despair.

When I meet someone who is hopeless, I grieve. The Good News of Jesus should be a welcome message to them because Jesus's life, death, and resurrection are **The Event** in history that conquers death, eradicates guilt and shame, and promises an eternity in heaven.

For people in Erikson's last stage, learning about the Holy Spirit can be a helpful strategy. When they let the Holy Spirit direct the course of their lives, amazing things start to happen. First, people hear God speaking to them, creating greater intimacy and richer **quiet times**. Second, God gives them the opportunities to **pray over** friends and to see people healed. Third, the Spirit will expand their viewpoint to bring the kingdom of God on earth, and infuse their daily routine with the breath of eternity. The Holy Spirit is the divine power source, working from within, that makes death lose its sting because He prepares people for heaven.

Spiritual Breathing

Let me point out how my **spiritual beliefs help me cope with my psychological problems**. My emotional issues often show up as "sin." Something has happened, and I've reacted poorly. The bottom line is that I've missed the mark of God's perfection. "Sinning" means that I have either done something *not pleasing to God* (a sin of commission), or I have *not* done something *God has asked me to do* (a sin of omission). Either way, I'm feeling guilty, ashamed, anxious, or depressed.

Here is how I recover from my missteps. First, I specifically confess how I have failed to do things God's way, and I ask His forgiveness in the name of Jesus.[143] Then, I call upon the Holy Spirit's power to change my behavior/attitude, and I thank Him for filling me.[144] Think of this process as breathing:[145] You breathe out the toxins, like CO_2 (i.e., empty self and repent), and breathe in the healthy, divine power, like oxygen (i.e., fill one's

---

143 1 John 1:9

144 Ephesians 5:18b

145 Nancy Wilson and Erik Segalini, "Use Spiritual Breathing to Surrender Control of Your Life to Christ | Cru," Cru.org, accessed May 22, 2019, https://www.cru.org/us/en/train-and-grow/help-others-grow/mentoring/spiritual-breathing-surrender-control.html.

self with the Holy Spirit). I repeat these two steps as often as necessary until I experience God's peace again. The peace of God is the referee in my heart.[146]

---

146 Colossians 3:15

PART FOUR:

BRIDGING FAITH
WITH EMOTIONAL HEALING

12
WAYS OF MANAGING SOUL PAIN

To REVIEW, MENTAL illness is a result of humanity's fundamental separation from the Creator. Because of this disconnection, evil entered our lives and, with it, our experiences of disease, dysfunction, and death. As we have read, both secular counselors and faith-based caregivers have much to offer anyone suffering with mental illness. In this final section, I will highlight the key concept: Our spiritual disconnect creates fear—and fear is the root of mental illness causing the soul to suffer. A personal relationship with Jesus is the key to managing soul pain because it reestablishes connection with God. Let's look more closely at how God suggests that we do this.

Mankind's suffering, due to our spirit's separation from God, deprives one of *feeling* God's love. In this condition, we stand exposed, afraid, and trembling. When we don't have God's protection, the enemy of our soul takes advantage of the cracks within us. These holes become Satan's entry points; specifically, the **stronghold** of fear turns into the enemy's primary weapon against us. For this reason, I believe it is wise to acknowledge the possibility of demonic activity in one's atmosphere. Fortunately, Jesus is our protective barrier against the enemy and his powers. Father God's perfect love wraps around us and helps us to overcome toxic realities in our souls, such as fear, shame, and a variety of traits we have associated with "mental illness."

To illustrate how faith is the solution to soul pain, I share how I have managed suffering. Then, I look briefly at how others have handled terrible times. Finally, I propose a psychology of suffering that I have found effective in my seasons of despair.

These suggestions may guide seekers back to a state of mental well-being.

My Wrestling Match With Shame and Guilt

Two years after I left my husband (and just three months after we were divorced), Rex announced that he had met a woman online and was going to marry her. The evening of their wedding, I decided "what is good for the gander, would be good for the goose." I went online to that same Christian dating site, signed in, and started hunting.

To make a long story short (please read my book, the *Heart of Deception*[147]), an Army major stationed in Afghanistan reached out to me. He courted me over the internet and via telephone. He said he would be retiring in about four months and returning to his suburban home, located one hour from me. He said a caretaker was watching the house for him. He was a widower and didn't have children.

He spoke my love language, knew how to ring my bells, and declared his love for me. He shared his Christian testimony. He quoted Scripture better than most people I know. He prayed with a powerful Christ-centered vocabulary. Over a period of six weeks, I fell hard for him.

So when he asked me (on the phone) to marry him when he returned to the States and retired, I was thrilled. We texted, messaged, and talked multiple times a day. A few days after his marriage proposal, he told me a friend of his, an Afghani sheikh, had just been killed, and had left him a chest of gold. He wanted to mail the heavy package to the United States before traveling home.

---

147 Julie Caton, *Heart of Deception: Cara Moore's True Story of an On-Line Dating Scam* (Batavia: Hi-Tek, 2014).

"This gold, honey, we'll use for the work of the Lord right there in Western New York," he said. That sounded good to me. I had been struggling with money for a long time, needed some to recover from my divorce, *and* I had a heart to help any Christian who needed it.

He continued, "So, would you please send me $10,000, to cover legal fees? I'll ship the gold right to you. When I get home, you'll get even more than your $10,000 back."

Two months had gone by since our courting started. I was *so happy* being loved and having someone to love. I was *so happy* being singled out as special, receiving love notes throughout the day, and having someone to talk to at night. Of course, I sent him the money. My desire for intimacy overrode any good sense I had.

Within two weeks of sending the money and his continuing to ask for more because of "shipping fees," a friend told me I was probably being deceived. So, the next day at sunrise, I drove for an hour to the address this long-distance "lover" had listed as his home. The whole time on the highway, my heart pounded. My hands perspired on the steering wheel.

I pulled up in front of his house at 7:00 a.m. When I saw children's toys cluttering the yard, my denial took a hit. Two station wagons, complete with child car seats, were parked in the driveway. Ouch! The hammer of truth painfully clobbered my denial again.

Then, across the street, I saw a man in police uniform arriving home from his nightshift. As he unlocked his front door, I crossed over to him, thrust a photo of my "fiancé" in front of his nose, and asked him, giving him the Army major's name, "Is this your neighbor?"

"Nope, I've never seen that dude in the photo before," the man said. That did it! My denial was shattered, crushed to smithereens. This alleged Army major had stolen someone's identity and address, put two months of effort into courting me under false pretenses, and scammed me out of my entire savings. He also broke my heart. Disgrace consumed me. Guilt lodged like a rock in my gut. Talk about soul pain!

Hot with shame, I drove home, fuming with anger. A spiritual wrestling match gripped me for the next day. Finally, the Lord took over. Thankfully, Jesus finally "pinned me," and won the match. I put God in the number one position in my life where He should have been all along, except that I had placed my husband and then my "long-distance lover" there instead. For nearly 50 years, I had walked with Christ as both my Lord and Savior. But I had not taken Jesus as my Betrothed, my spiritual husband. Now, in my current wounded condition, I needed someone to fill my emotional core. So, I released my overwhelming shame to Jesus. I rolled over the guilt of my mistake to Him. And I recommitted myself to the Son of God at a much deeper level than I ever had before.

This healing process changed how I related to Jesus. During my evenings, when previously I had been on the phone with the scam man, now I would read the Bible. Instead of thinking about the scammer throughout the day, now I talked out loud to Jesus, whispering words of love. I even started "texting" Jesus, almost like I had done with the scammer, which was a form of two-way journaling.[148]

After the problems from the scam settled down, I realized I had learned an important lesson: I knew how I *felt* when I had been "in love." Now, I could capture that same love experience with Jesus. So I entered into a **soul bond** with the LORD that helped me to love Him emotionally, and in turn, to *feel* His love for me through the Holy Spirit. In my **quiet times** with Jesus, I would go into the "**secret chamber**" to meditate, and become wrapped up in His Presence. This God-given love reduced my fears.

---

148 Mark and Patti Virkler, *Four Keys to Hearing God's Voice* (Shippensburg: Destiny Image Publishers, 2010).

The Auction Block
by Julie Caton

I'm shoved up onto the slave block,
Someone's property,
So hands reach up
To poke and prod my flesh, my thighs, the soles of my feet,
Assessing my value.
Heat rises up my neck,
Though my naked body shivers.
Shackles chaff my ankles.
I cannot hide my shame.

The auctioneer hawks his wares:
"What is she worth?"
"What is she good for?"
"Who will buy this female slave?"
Naked, cowering female.

The crowd mumbles, coughs, shoves, jeers, bids, spits.
Gavel pounds the auction block.
SOLD
Into captivity
AGAIN.

My new master steps forward and does the extraordinary:
He covers my nakedness with his own cloak.
He unlocks my leg fetters.
He signs the document,
And he hands me my papers,
MAKING ME FREE.
My freedom papers!
I am emancipated!
I AM REDEEMED! He has purchased me out of slavery!

Today I remember that precious moment,
the minute I was set free.
And whenever I make a mistake,
I take it to my Master to be redeemed,
Just like I had been.
My redeemer buys my error off the slave block.
He sets me free from my mistakes again and again and again and again
and again and again and...

My Wrestling Match With Fear

During two different experiences, occurring 25 years apart, I struggled with significant fear. The first of these was during my psychology internship in a city hospital. The second snuck up on me after the scam, in 2014. In both cases, weeping became the outlet for my pain.

During the internship, I was deeply afraid of my failing the psychology program, and thus failing myself. While working as an intern, I was teased for my faith and criticized for my attitude. I was being trained by a team of nine arrogant psychologists, including the chief, a resentful man who supervised me with near-paranoid vigilance. A long day at the hospital involved treating severely disturbed patients, writing psychological evaluations, and sitting through disparaging supervision sessions. In the evening, I would drive the one-hour commute home and sniffle back tears as I reviewed the day.

In the midst of these difficulties, Rex, who disapproved of my participation in the doctoral program, offered little support. On the few occasions I complained about the hospital's training, Rex would say, "Why don't you just quit? I told you this wouldn't work." My soul pain increased.

My fear of rejection was deep and pervasive. I recall that year as being one of the toughest of my life. Because I was ashamed of the possibility of failure, I stopped talking to anyone about my feelings. No one understood what I was going through. Yes, I knew Jesus loved me, and I took time to study the Bible and pray. But I did not *feel* the Holy Spirit's love during that year.

Emotionally, the second-hardest season of my life happened four years after I left the marriage. By that time, the dust of divorce had settled. I had recovered from the scam (or so I thought). I was attending a very small, Spirit-filled church, where the pastor taught about the Holy Spirit. I had experienced the miraculous healing from the bike accident. I had a circle of supportive friends who were receiving their own healings and

gifts of the Spirit. My clinical patients were calling on the Holy Spirit, whose power had been introduced as part of their healing.

Despite all of that, in early September 2014, I became emotionally unstable and began to weep for no good reason. Sobs would just flow up from my soul. I couldn't stop them. If no one was around, I would lie on the floor for hours and cry. If a scheduled client arrived, I just sucked it up, washed my face, and pretended everything was fine.

The crying jags started the day I happened upon old text messages from the scammer buried in my phone. So, I started to delete anything on my phone connected to him, and I began to cry. Was I releasing more shame? I was okay with that. Those tears seemed appropriate. Truly, my heart had been broken.

But the weeping continued day and night. I became afraid of these uncontrollable tears. Would my crying ever stop? I sought explanations. Was this a result of physical fatigue, residue of the divorce stress? Was I crying because of the onset of winter and perhaps had **Seasonal Affective Disorder**? When I was still crying several weeks later, I said to myself, "Oh, this must be a premature grieving for my 97-year-old mother's upcoming death." She was one tough, determined lady who was declining further and further into dementia. Every three months, I would visit her in Florida and find that her body and soul had "died" a little more. (Mom passed into heaven six months later.)

In retrospect, my experience of suffering from this excessive weeping was distinctly different from that of my internship year. This time, I was living in an emotionally healthy environment, compared to the toxic experience of my failing marriage. This time, Christian friends comforted me when I expressed shame about my ceaseless crying. My pastor prayed with me. The Holy Spirit was growing in me, and I enjoyed His daily comfort. I had cultivated an active love relationship with Jesus because of lessons I had learned from the scam. This love sustained me.

As one month of weeping turned into a second month and then a third month, I stopped questioning the tears and began to embrace them. **I claimed the Scripture**: "As they pass through the Valley of Baka (weeping), they make it a place of springs...."[149] I gave into the crying. Friends said, "You need to cleanse yourself emotionally. Go ahead and cry." Some would hold me while I wept. I used certain songs and hymns as expressions of my lament. I praised the Lord in the midst of the sobbing. Indeed, God was using my tears as a lens cleaner on my view of life, helping me to see things *His* way.

During this season, I also had random bouts of vertigo and nausea. At the end of November 2014, I awoke in the middle of the night needing to vomit. The experience I'm going to describe has been a turning point in my life. I got on my knees and began heaving in the toilet. Then, I did something I'd never done before—I praised the Lord while I was vomiting. For the next few hours, I would repeatedly heave and praise the Lord. It was a breakthrough for me, and my season of weeping ceased that night. I believe I had been releasing spiritual darkness for the previous few months, and this last bout of sickness cast all toxic presences out, once and for all.

What did I learn about adversity from these two different experiences? Going through suffering alone is much harder than facing pain while friends support you. That is why the Body of Christ (the church) plays an important role in helping Christ-ones (Christians) endure suffering. When I was in my internship (1990), I had limited human support. However, when I was going through my struggle in 2014, people embraced me, encouraged me, and let me weep on them. This blessing of fellowship was crucial in helping me ease my pain and fear. I also learned the importance and power of praising God *even when I did not feel*

---

149 Psalm 84:6

like it. The enemy runs from our praise of the Almighty God—
don't ever forget that.[150]

Ways in Which People Handle Suffering

One day when I was thinking about God's love and the
psychology of suffering, a Voice of the Martyrs (VOM) email
flew across my computer screen. I had been wondering: How
does God's love address fear? Would it help to hear how people
handle their suffering? How did they incorporate perfect love
when embroiled in adversity?

Over the years, I have joined in the suffering of many
people, whether through personal contact, reading their memoirs,
or watching a documentary about them. What follow are poignant
examples:

- A mentally confused woman who was returned to the
  hospital for the third time with an undiagnosed systemic
  infection
- A pregnant mother carrying her baby to term even though
  doctors had said the unborn would die of a heart defect
  once born
- The grandfather-to-be who was bedridden with Lou
  Gehrig's disease and heartbroken that his failing lung
  muscles would likely cause his death before he'd be able
  to see his grandson

Each of these people had discovered the presence of God
within their souls. I had the privilege of seeing them push into His
love, which cast their fears away.

Petr Jasek's Story

A particular Voice of the Martyrs's email piqued my
interest. The story was about a middle-aged Czech, Petr Jasek,

---

150 Psalm 8:2

who had been released from a Sudanese prison after a 14-month incarceration. Petr, a staff member of VOM, had entered Sudan to assist members of the **Persecuted Church**. Just as he was leaving, he was detained and held in jail on bogus charges of espionage and treason. He inhabited a small cell with six ISIS Muslims who treated him as a slave.

How did Petr cope with the suffering he endured? How did he manage the depression that overcame him when he thought about his family? What did he do with the daily anxiety rattling his soul as he waited for his sentencing?[151]

During his interview with VOM Radio host, Todd Nettleton, Petr shared several keys to how he handled his ordeal. To ward off his anxiety, the Holy Spirit suggested Petr recite Scripture, particularly Revelation 4:8:

> Each of the four living creatures [around God's throne] had six wings and was covered with eyes all around, even under its wings. Day and night they never stop saying: "Holy, holy, holy is the Lord God Almighty, who was, and is, and is to come."

Petr challenged himself to repeat those words of worship unceasingly during his suffering.

When Petr prayed, thoughts of his wife and children made him weep. Yet, Petr had to maintain his emotional control because of the cruel attitude of his cellmates, so he chose not to pray for his family. But when the cellmates started torturing him, Petr used this window of opportunity to cry, to mourn, and to grieve because his cellmates now expected his tears of anguish.

---

151 "Petr Jasek: Prisoner Set Free," VOM Radio (audio blog), March 17, 2017, accessed June 23, 2018, VOMRadio.net;

"Petr Jasek: The Greatest Peace," VOM Radio (audio blog), March 24, 2017, accessed June 23, 2018, VOMRadio.net;

"Petr Jasek: God Opened the Door," VOM Radio (audio blog), March 30, 2017, accessed June 23, 2018, VOMRadio.net.

So he went ahead and prayed freely, declaring the glory of God, praising the Lord in worship, and weeping.

Also, Petr focused his thoughts on Jesus. When his thoughts were on his Savior, he would feel God's presence, even during the beatings. During Petr's ordeal, his breakthrough moments came when he was able to connect with the love of God. He reported experiencing intimacy with God and divine love when he was worshipping, meditating, reading Scripture, and sharing in the sufferings of his fellow inmates. When he focused on the Almighty Who Is Love, Petr found that his emotional suffering evaporated.

Immaculée Ilibagiza's Story

Immaculée Ilibagiza shares her story of pain and suffering in her book, *Left To Tell*.[152] At the time of the outbreak of the Rwandan genocide in 1994, she was a Tutsi college student. Immaculée was hidden in a tiny bathroom with six other women for three months in order to avoid the murderous rage of the blood-thirsty Hutus. God honored her devotion to Him. She used her time in hiding to pray the rosary (her father's gift), to tell herself Bible stories, to intercede for her loved ones, and to wrestle with God in prayer. She learned to forgive and love her enemies. She enjoyed praising the Lord. God blessed her with spiritual strength, revelations, and an occasional vision to succor her during her ordeal. Throughout her writings, Immaculée refers to the intimate times of loving on God and being loved by Him as the solution to her pain.

Joni Eareckson Tada's View of Suffering

Joni Eareckson Tada, a Christian woman about my age, had a diving accident in 1967 that broke her neck. Within seconds,

---

152 Immaculée Ilibagiza, *Left To Tell: Discovering God Amidst the Rwandan Holocaust* (Carlsbad: Hay House, 2006).

she became a spinal-cord-injured, quadriplegic; she has been in a wheelchair ever since. Joni shared an insight into her affliction: "Suffering involves having what you do not want, and wanting what you do not have."[153] She addressed the primary question: "Why do I have to suffer?"

Joni shared that by changing her attitude toward hardship, she began to see how her quadriplegia was working for her good and God's glory. "I realized that being paralyzed was making heaven come alive—not in a cop-out way, but in a way that made me want to live better here on earth because greater things were coming in the next life."[154] Also, Joni reminded me that "the Son of God did not exempt Himself from affliction, but lived through it and learned from it."[155]

The last chapter of this book provides a "psychology of suffering" to use as a guide for anyone in need. In my effort to create a psychological strategy for managing emotional pain, I do not want to minimize suffering in any way. Suffering is *the most challenging place* to be. Nevertheless, I make this effort because I want to reduce suffering in our world—both its frequency and its intensity. We givers, whether secular or faith-based, often overlook important factors influencing mental illness. Hopefully, these practical steps on managing suffering will benefit you. I pray that seekers will find answers in the lessons I've learned.

---

153 Joni Eareckson Tada, *Making Sense of Suffering* (Peabody: Aspire Press, 2012), 2-7.

154 Ibid.

155 Ibid.

13
A FRESH LOOK AT RESPONDING TO SOUL PAIN

SOUL PAIN MAY appear as symptoms of depression or anxiety; problems in relationships or daily functioning; or bizarre thinking or overwhelming thought patterns. It may come clothed in anger, weeping, panic, or gut pain. The person who is suffering typically responds in one or more of these five ways:

- A typical first choice may be to ignore the symptoms and bury the problem. Sadly, this causes the pain to get worse.
- The person may use a "medication" of choice, whether it is doctor-prescribed (like Prozac) or one he finds "on the street" (like marijuana or alcohol).
- The sufferer might respond by indulging in a dysfunctional behavior. He could become a workaholic, shopaholic, chocoholic, or even church-aholic.
- He might call a clinical therapist and "spill his guts," hoping that the art of psychotherapy will cure him.
- His final choice might be to seek out faith-based pastoral care workers and request healing prayer.

Seekers might be motivated to do all of the above.

Faith in God Is the Best Response to Pain

Among the variety of ways in which people respond to soul pain, each person has the right to choose what seems best. In my opinion, **faith in God is the best answer to soul pain**. It is the reason why I wrote this book.

Let me throw out a challenge. To the people who have unrelenting soul pain, try this gamble: Say, "If faith in God is the answer to my pain (as this book and these testimonies declare), then, God, I ask You to show me Yourself, Your love, Your solution." Simply open a crack in your confused soul, and let the light and love of God shine in. See what happens. What can you lose?

The following reasons summarize why **faith in God is the solution to soul pain**:

❖ God made man in His own image.[156] Thus, human beings were created to connect with God. But the "fall" caused a separation between man and God. **Faith in the Almighty restores that connection**, which is the foundational purpose of one's life as God designed it. When disconnection happens, the person becomes less than he was created to be.

❖ We live in a world that is fallen, sinful, corrupt, and toxic. Thus, a human being needs an **available power source** to combat all of this spiritual darkness. Faith in Jesus Christ, the Overcomer, gives us the **victory over evil**.[157]

❖ Human beings are vulnerable to sickness, trauma, and injuries, both physical and emotional. Faith in God as the Holy Spirit is the **platform for healing**[158] in the name of Jesus.

❖ At the heart of soul pain is the emotion of fear. Fear's most fundamental effect is to make a person afraid of pain and death. Faith in Jesus—who suffered, died, and was

---

156 Genesis 1:27

157 John 16:33; 1 John 5:4

158 Acts 10:38

resurrected—overcomes **one's fear of suffering and dying.**[159]

When I entered the field of psychology, I hoped to find answers to some existential questions, such as "Why does suffering occur?" "What's the purpose of pain?" "How can we solve the problem of pain?"

Forty years later I report this to you: *I have not found answers to these questions in the field of psychology*—but *I have come close to finding them in Jesus.*

Jesus has taught me a psychology of suffering, which involves overcoming the fear of death.

Fear Is the Root of Soul Pain

Do you agree that one's psychological pain stems from fear? People's fears take on different forms—fear of failure, intimacy, physical pain, or loss of control. However, the foundational cause of fear is our fear of death. "Death" is more than just physical demise. Death is a complete loss of control. It is a fear of one being annihilated, or having no voice, of being utterly alone. It is a fear of the complete unknown, a profound nothingness, an eternal void.

Fear is at the root of most problems. To understand that statement, try this:

1. If you are participating in therapy, take whatever problem is on the table and deconstruct it. To "deconstruct it," keep asking yourself: "What's so bad about such-and-such (insert a label for your problem)?"

2. Then, take that answer and apply the same question.

3. Push to the root. Keep going deeper.

---

159 1 Corinthians 15:56-57

4. The answer will factor down to "I'm afraid of
_____ (fill in the blank)."

As an example, let's deconstruct the motives for my blindly entering into a relationship with someone on the internet who eventually scammed me.

My therapist might ask: "Why did you seek out a man whom you barely knew?"

My answer: "Because I was afraid of being alone for the rest of my life."

Therapist: "Why are you afraid of being alone for the rest of your life?"

Answer: "Because I feel terrible when I am completely by myself; I'm afraid something is missing."

Therapist: "Why do you fear that something is missing?"

Answer: (Exasperated sigh) "I don't know! It's just a deep pain. It just feels like something is wrong. Like I'm nothing. I can't explain it."

Fear is man's bottom-line emotion. When we try to help people with soul pain, we must deal with their most fundamental problem—that of fear, particularly fear of death. Thus, eradicating fear is the key to my proposed psychology of suffering.

You may have heard of Dr. Chauncey Crandall IV, and how the Lord has blessed his cardiology practice—even to the point of God using him to bring a man back to life.[160] On September 20, 2006, 53-year-old Jeff Markin arrived at the emergency room with chest pains, collapsed from a massive heart attack, and, within an hour, died on the operating room table. Dr. Crandall

---

160 "Dr. Chauncey Crandall: A Patient Raised from the Dead," CBN.com, April 13, 2015, accessed January 15, 2019, http://www1.cbn.com/content/dr-chauncey-crandall-patient-raised-dead.

records this exciting testimony in his book *Raising the Dead*.[161] In the following paragraphs, I excerpt sections of that book and share the end of Mr. Markin's story. His experience while dead illustrates what death might be like, and why we fear it.

> *Jeff Markin came back to life on a Friday and spent the weekend in the ICU recovering from being dead. On Monday, Dr. Crandall asked him, "I'm curious. What was it like when you died?"*

> *Jeff answered: "I'm so disappointed...no one came to visit me...I was in a casket in a dark room for eternity—hell, okay? I sat there alone. After being there for eternity, some men came in, and they wrapped me up and threw me in the trash."*

Jeff's vision was of final separation—a total waste of his life. Dr. Crandall encouraged Jeff to accept the Lord as his Savior and said, "You will never again be thrown in the trash when you become born again."

Skeptics may not believe in their heads that death is total separation from the all-loving God, which is hell. But I think that in their hearts they know the truth of this reality, and it kicks up an existential fear—our fear of death—which is at the root of most of our emotional problems.

The Dawn of Fear

Let's revisit Adam and Eve in the Garden of Eden at the very beginning when there was no fear. Adam was the Creator's first living being. Together, God and man enjoyed the luxuries of Paradise. Adam was surrounded by starry galaxies, sunrises and sunsets, beautiful plants, and luscious food. He had gardens to till, rivers to fish, and trees from which to pluck fruit. He had the company of animals and birds, and finally, he had his lovely helpmate, Eve. Adam and Eve felt love because the God Who Is

---

161 Chauncey Crandall IV. *Raising the Dead* (New York: FaithWords, 2010), 187-193.

187

Love lived right there with them. They were naked and experienced no shame and no fear.

Then, Eve disobeyed the heavenly Father because of her pride, and she ate the apple. Adam also disobeyed God. Why did Adam disobey? I think he was afraid. If he didn't agree with Eve and join her by eating his half of the apple, she might reject him. Maybe she scolded him and said, "Because you don't want to do things my way, I don't want to have anything to do with you." We really don't know for sure. But Adam's fear? If he didn't comply with Eve's request, she'd be angry and leave him. He'd be alone. If no Eve, then no tangible love.

Thus, sin entered the world in the forms of disobedience, shame, and fear.[162] This story reveals the first time that the word "afraid" is used in Scripture. The concept of "fear" (or some form of it) appears more than 500 times in the Bible. Twenty-three times, Jesus said to His followers, "Fear not. Do not be afraid."

Fear, the root cause of our suffering, is triggered by pain. When my wrist and ribs were fractured, the physical pain was intolerable at times, and I felt fear. When I was scammed and my heart was broken, the emotional pain overwhelmed me, and I felt fear. My suffering resulted from both pain and fear.

So, then, if fear is the cause of suffering, what is the answer to mankind's fear?

God tells us that perfect love is the antidote to fear. "There is no fear in love. But perfect love drives out fear."[163] So, does it follow that this love is the answer to suffering? Could God's love be the solution to our soul pain and the cure to mental illness?

---

162 Genesis 3:10

163 1 John 4:18

Suffering Originates From the Dark Side

When studying soul pain and its companion of suffering, I find a culprit lurking behind that door. We've read that fear and pain hurt people when mental or physical disease debilitates their lives. We've heard testimonies about man's inhumanity to man. I believe the root source of suffering is a willful, intelligent spirit called the devil. He made his appearance after Adam and Eve, healthy in all ways, were created. The Scripture introduces the serpent, the most crafty of all creatures, as he sets out to disrupt man's idyllic paradise by tempting Eve to take control of her own life. "You will not certainly die…you will be like God," the serpent said.[164]

Please note that this serpent, once a beautiful angel called the Morning Star,[165] was exiled from heaven by the Almighty God. The reason for his expulsion? The rebel angel had said, "I will make myself equal to God." And since that time, the heart of man, because of his fallen nature, has had little (or no) respect for the Lord.[166]

This embodiment of evil is recognized by most world religions. In the Judeo-Christian tradition, this fallen angel, "Lucifer" (Satan), was given freedom to reign on this earth as the Prince of the World. The devil's game plan? To kill, steal, and destroy anything that makes an imprint for the kingdom of God on earth. The enemy instigates mental illness and creates havoc by corrupting us with bad habits and wretched spirits.

Just the other day, I was counseling a single mother and her teenage daughter for their sixth session in six months. A breach in their relationship had caused them pain and had brought them into therapy. The girl was being independent, uncooperative, and rebellious. Often, the mother cried or scolded because of her

---

164 Genesis 3:4-5

165 Isaiah 14:12, 14

166 Isaiah 5:12, 24

daughter's attitude. Certainly, their mutual reactions worsened the problem.

That day, I met with them individually to assess the atmosphere. I asked each of them (alone) how important God was in her life. The daughter said privately to me, "Not much. Oh, we go to Christmas Mass once a year." Fifteen minutes later, the mother, also alone with me, said the same thing. When the three of us were together at the end of the session, I asked them, "If I told you that having faith in God would help you through this mess, would you be interested?"

In unison, they said, "No, thanks. I don't need God."

I grieve for them and for all people who are not asking for God's help. The upcoming generation conveys this attitude: "I want my children to choose whatever they want, whatever behavior, sexual orientation, ethical code, life philosophy that they want. I'm their parent, but I want them to be free. I will not be their authority, nor will I encourage them to embrace the Creator God and His Holy Scriptures as their authority. They should have control of their own lives."

To reduce emotional pain, we need to reverse this pattern and declare: "Jesus, I'm sorry. I have considered myself equal to You. I've made myself my own God, my own boss. What a mess! Please forgive me through Jesus Christ. Please come into my heart and reconnect with me. I want You as Lord, so I can live with You in the sweet spot of Your will. I ask this in Jesus's name, Amen."

The Problem of Signature Sin

One of my seekers had severe trouble with anger. After weeks of "talk therapy," we were at a loss because there was no improvement. Mack, a recovered alcoholic, had shown outbursts of anger for a good number of years. After he committed himself to Jesus, he still couldn't break the behavior of lashing out at family or bursting with road rage. To reduce the anger, we used clinical techniques for several months but made little progress.

Together, we raised the question: Might Mack be oppressed by a demon of rage? So, I asked a team of pastors experienced in delivering people from this kind of oppression.

One of the pastors suggested a different take on Mack's emotional issue.

"Maybe Mack has developed a signature sin of anger.[167] When things didn't go his way as an abused child, he got angry, right? Now, he does it more out of habit than anything else. But we'll talk to him," the pastor said.

Honestly, Mack and I were hopeful that there would be some spiritual presence provoking him to anger, which the pastors could identify. It would be an "easy" solution to find a stronghold of anger and throw it away. But that was not what happened.

There were two outcomes to this story.

Once challenged with the idea that his anger was a "signature sin" (i.e., a chronic habit and not a negative stronghold), Mack began to accept responsibility for his behavior. No longer able to say, "Oh the devil made me do it," he works hard to manage his outbursts, to spend more time with Jesus, and to fill his soul with Scripture. He is recognizing the roots of his soul pain, which were childhood fears because he was abused, and he is bringing them to the Lord for inner healing.

The second result was my opportunity to hear the testimony of one of the two pastors. Pastor R.L., raised in a spiritually oppressive environment, struggled with depression and suicidal ideation even before he recognized the extent to which he needed deliverance. To manage his soul pain, he tried self-cutting as a way of soothing himself. He hoped that feeling the pain of the

---

167 Michael Mangis, *Signature Sins: Taming Our Wayward Hearts* (Downers Grove: InterVarsity Press, 2008).

slice and seeing the blood would release the toxic emotions stirring within him.

Pastor R.L.'s Testimony: It's All About Deliverance

I grew up in a small village in Western New York, and in sixth grade, I made friends with a classmate who came from a private community called Lily Dale. Lily Dale was a settlement (dating back to 1879) of Spiritists and Freethinkers that had become the largest center of the Spiritualist movement hosting over 22,000 visitors annually.

The boy began telling me about his spirit guides and his father's role as a trumpet medium within the community. At that age, I was fascinated by but also leery of it, as I had been attending a youth group at my grandmother's church. Although I wasn't a believer yet, I knew the stuff I had been discovering didn't really fit with what I had been learning in the Bible.

*Throughout high school, I was depressed with suicidal thoughts and took to cutting. A lot of changes took place, including my friend's conversion to Christianity and my experimenting with **meditation** and healing crystals. One of my high school professors had us participate in meditation at the beginning of every class by using intense breathing exercises and out-of-body experiences. I did not realize it at the time, but he was also a leader at Lily Dale.*

After we graduated, I took a bus to a college in Kansas, where I roomed with this friend from school. My motives? To run away from a broken relationship with my father and to explore what being a Christian really meant.

Even while I learned more about Christ and desired to live for Him, something held me back. In spite of my new devotion to God, I continued some of the practices I had learned, including meditation. I had been taught that as long as you go into meditation with good thoughts, you would only connect with good spirits, so I justified my doing it. I kept an amethyst healing crystal around my neck.

One evening when I was meditating, my roommate walked in. He said, "What you are doing is no different from what my family had done back in Lily Dale. I'm concerned for you." As soon as he left the room, I stopped what I was doing and cried out to God to forgive me and deliver me. That's when I realized I was in a spiritual battle.

Later that night after we had turned the lights off and gone to bed, strange things started to happen. Since we had an inner room, one with no windows, it was always very dark. But this night it felt even darker. No sooner had my roommate flipped the light off than I felt paralyzed on top of my bed. Something like a shadow, even darker than the darkness, began to hover over me. Then, there was a sudden flicker of light as my amethyst crystal, laying on my desk, began to glow.

I could neither speak nor move. Thankfully, my roommate realized immediately what was going on and started to cry out, "Leave in the name of Jesus!" He jumped down from his loft and turned on the light. This act dispelled the darkness and allowed me to speak and move again. But everything felt just as eerie and cold.

Quickly, we began praying together, and within five minutes, an older ministry student from another dorm showed up, uninvited. Instinctively, he came in and began praying. Soon after, others joined him. By 2 a.m., things felt "normal" again. After everyone had left, my roommate and I took the crystal from my desk, went outside, and smashed it with large rocks.

The next morning, I was called into the Office of the College President and found him to be both knowledgeable of and compassionate toward my situation. He walked with me back to my room and began to reveal to me tons of symbols, inscribed on wall hangings and formed in jewelry, that I hadn't even realized I had owned. After he left, I began collecting everything together, along with music and movies that I felt were not good influences. That night, my roommate and I had a bonfire and got rid of all the "junk."

It was soon after that, with a clean and right spirit, I gave myself 100 percent to Christ and received His call on my life to minister in His name. That is what I have been doing ever since.

Pastor R. L., Western New York

When dealing with psychiatric problems, one needs to be discerning, as you can see from these stories. Not all mental illness is demonically caused; it could just as easily have its roots in neurological or chemical dysfunction. Recently, I spoke with cardiologist Dr. Chauncey Crandall, who is adept at distinguishing between the two realms. He asks himself: "Does the problem originate in the supernatural and spiritual aspects of the seeker's life, or are there bio-psycho-social causes at the root?"

To illustrate this idea, I share a case adapted from his book, *Touching Heaven.*

Dr. Crandall's Complex Case of Sarah

When I met Sarah in my office, she handed me medical documents revealing her story of recurrent seizures, from which she had gotten little to no relief. During our appointment, I spent time learning the origin of her seizures. For years, growing up, she had been raped by male relatives and would make herself go into a trance, or create pseudo-seizures, to get the men to stop. In addition to this behavior, her trauma history had opened the door to more sinister problems.

After our interview, I left the exam office, and within minutes, my assistant rushed out behind me: "Doctor, she's having a full-blown seizure right now!" I discerned instantly that these weren't seizures, but demons. "Go get my Bible!" I said to my assistant. I put the Bible on Sarah's belly and prayed to rebuke the spirits that were there. Sarah stopped seizing immediately.

Believing the demons had vacated, I started writing my chart notes. But Sarah started to have a seizure again. After about 90 minutes of struggling with her, multiple attempts at using anti-seizure medication, and seeing my staff's heightened concern, I thought: Maybe this is flesh-driven, meaning the effects of old habits that she had used to cope with the abuse were at play. Because these psychological mechanisms are an individual's choice—i.e., natural, protective responses to trauma—they can be helped by medical means. So, we quickly had her transferred to a psychiatric hospital.

Three months later, Sarah came back to thank me for praying, and I saw a new person, inside and out. She confirmed that she had come to know Christ while at the psychiatric hospital and that she was also cured of her seizures.

Intrigued, I asked her: "What happened that day?"

Sarah said, "Doc, I was loaded with demons, and the last one was cast out when you prayed."

I've been asked if I'm afraid in these situations. Not anymore. I am well aware of the power of darkness, but I live and work under a far greater power, and so I know I never have to be afraid. All of the weapons of hell are powerless against me as long as I am covered under the blood of Christ, walking in the might of heaven, and wielding the sword of the Spirit, which is the Word of God.[168]

---

168 Chauncey Crandall IV and Kris Bearss, *Touching Heaven: A Cardiologist's Encounters With Death and Living Proof of an Afterlife* (New York: FaithWords, 2015), 87-89.

14

IF SUFFERING COMES FROM THE ENEMY, WE NEED DELIVERANCE MINISTRY

IN THE LAST few years, I have gained awareness of the spiritual world and the dark forces influencing our fears and pain. I sense the spiritual battle around me, in my clients, and in the population at large. Because I desire to bring emotional healing to seekers, I have continued learning about inner and physical healing, and have studied the topic of deliverance.

Deliverance was the part of Jesus's ministry when He cast out demons and broke off spiritual strongholds from people.[169] Up until three years ago, I minimized spiritual warfare, thinking it was an abstract, doctrinal construct. Now I know there is a spiritual realm on this earth under the domain of the devil.[170] It's populated with demons that have intelligence, emotions, willfulness, and assignments from hell. They desire to shackle us with strongholds of various kinds—lies we believe, curses handed down to us from our ancestors, soul ties that stifle our growth, wounds of the heart, and chronic illness, to list a few.[171] Jesus described the enemy, Satan, as a purposeful thief targeting human beings so that we suffer.[172]

---

169 Mark 9:25-26; Luke 8:29

170 John 12:31; 2 Corinthians 4:4

171 Peter Horrobin, *Healing through Deliverance: Foundation and Practice of Deliverance Ministry* (Grand Rapids, MI: Chosen Books, 2008), 73-80; 95-119.

See also: Derek Prince, *They Shall Expel Demons* (Grand Rapids: Chosen Books, 1998).

172 John 10:10

Restoring the Foundations

A few years ago, I wanted to be sure that no such demonic attachments were disrupting the work of God in my life, an important goal if I wanted to help others find their emotional health. For that reason, I signed up for a "freedom weekend" through a ministry called Restoring the Foundations. A compassionate, well-trained, and spiritually mature couple ministered to me over three days (i.e., 15 hours), examining my ancestral history, my relationship difficulties, times I had been victimized, my religious practices, my emotional upheavals, and my thought life. You name it, and we addressed it. When the counselors perceived demonic connection to an area of my life, we renounced it. With each confession and each rebuke, an evil stronghold was broken off me. Breath by breath, shackle by shackle, the bonds were released.

I experienced increasing nausea as our sessions progressed and had to stop a few times to let my stomach settle. The counselors told me that typically, when demons are expelled, the believer feels nauseous, burpy, flatulent, or sleepy. Or, the person might start coughing, yawning, or experiencing an unexplained, sudden pain. When my freedom weekend was complete, I felt emotionally exhausted and spiritually liberated. It was one of the best uses of my time and money ever!

Paula's Deliverance

Two weeks after my own deliverance experience, I had my first personal encounter with someone else's demon in my home office. An attractive, blonde, middle-aged grandmother, Paula, arrived for her monthly appointment. She had been coming to me for five years because she was highly anxious and somewhat paranoid. Her symptoms had resulted from a sexual assault by a man in a public ladies' room. Until this point, we had used "talk therapy," including deep breathing and stress relief, and had followed basic biblical teachings. Paula had built a solid soul bond with Jesus, but she continued to struggle with anxiety.

At the start of this particular session, per usual, she sat down on my office couch, and I sat opposite her on my desk chair. We caught up on the details of her life and how she was doing. Then, she said, "I want to know more about the Holy Spirit, things like you told me the last time." Paula attended the same charismatic church I did. She had heard my testimony of the Holy Spirit healing my fractured wrist and had learned about being **anointed in the Spirit**. She was hungry for a deeper walk with Jesus.

We reviewed more of the doctrine of the Holy Spirit. Then, Paula asked, "Can I receive the **gift of tongues**?" ("Tongues," or *glossolalia,* is the God-given gift that allows the person to speak in a heavenly language. The practice brings spiritual refreshment and empowerment to the praying person.[173])

"We certainly can pray for that gift. The Father loves to give the gifts of the Holy Spirit to His children," I said.

After saying that, I stood next to her and, with her permission, laid my hand on her head. I asked the Lord to anoint her with the Holy Spirit. She began to utter something from her mouth, and I thought the Lord was giving her the gift of tongues.

Suddenly, Paula began to choke. Her eyes bulged, and she put her hands to her throat. At that moment, the Lord gave me the knowledge that a demon had seized her. Fortunately, from my recent Bible readings, I knew what was happening and what I should do.

"Be quiet," I said firmly, addressing the presence. "Leave her alone. Go away now, in the name of Jesus." I sat down next to Paula. She turned and glared at me.

This time her voice was deep, guttural, and masculine, and said, "Who are you? You don't belong here." That was definitely a demonic voice.

---

173 For more about *glossolalia*, read 1 Corinthians 12 and 14, and the book of Acts.

Once again, I said, "Quiet. Stop, in the name of Jesus." Then, there was silence.

Shaking her head as she came out of her daze, Paula drew a breath and asked, "What happened?"

"I think that was a demon," I said. "It didn't want you to receive the gift of tongues." She and I had been listening to our pastor talk about demons so this was not too shocking to her. Immediately, we called our pastor, who assured us we had handled the situation correctly. Paula would be okay, and we could meet the next day and get rid of it.

Our pastor came with his wife, and within five minutes, as the four of us prayed, Paula began to choke again. She gagged a few times, and her facial features were strained. After a minute of dry retching, she coughed out something. Her face then changed, and she settled into a state of relaxed joy. She and I saw no physical manifestation of "it," but our pastor discerned what type of demon it was and called it "fear." This was no surprise to me, as I had been treating Paula for fear and paranoia ever since she had been attacked. Along with spiritual freedom, she received her heavenly language that day.

Most of us don't talk about these happenings. Nevertheless, people have spoken to me about the discomfort they feel when they became aware of such dark-side activities, such as seeing wisps of darkness or glowing eyes, or hearing scary voices in their presence, among other strange sensory experiences. In truth, we all need to take these spirit presences seriously.

The Doctrine of Deliverance in a Nutshell

It is important to know biblical principles to equip our toolboxes for the spiritual battle. When it comes to breaking free spiritually from evil, the core doctrines include:

1. Jesus's death defeated Satan and his demons.[174]

2. On the cross, Jesus stripped Satan of all power. His power is finite and has an expiration date.[175]

3. The Holy Spirit has been given to Christian believers, and with that gift, God has given us the **authority** to cast away any dark spirits.[176]

4. Christ's blood is our protection,[177] and while we wear the armor of God,[178] nothing can prevail against us that is not permitted to do so by the heavenly Father.

Satan indeed prowls around trying to nip at us or even bite us until we bleed. He looks for chinks in our spiritual armor to sneak in and wreak havoc. However, the devil is stopped dead in his tracks and is turned away when we use the powerful weapons of praise for the Almighty and invoking Jesus's name.[179] At an emotional level, fear is cast away when we focus on God's perfect love.[180] Praying in the authority Jesus has given us is a surefire way of winning spiritual battles.

When faith-based seekers battle problems with addictions, anger, and anxiety, or have trauma histories, givers should discuss this additional aspect of ministry—their deliverance. Many of my clients have benefitted from praying a "bondage-breaking" prayer with me to experience freedom from whatever is causing them pain. The prayer takes them through the basic steps of confessing their problem, forgiving themselves or their ancestors for causing the problem, and then disavowing their involvement with that specific culprit. We then command the spirit of evil (i.e., the

---

174 Hebrews 2:14

175 Colossians 2:15

176 Luke 9:1; Matthew 18:18

177 Revelation 12:10

178 Ephesians 6:10-17

179 Psalm 8:2; Acts 3:16

180 1 John 4:18

stronghold) to leave and cast it away. Finally, we thank God for exchanging a kingdom of God resource to take the place of the "stronghold." For example, if we cast away fear, we exchange it for God's love. This simple way of praying has reduced symptoms in clients quickly and effectively.

Suggested Prayer for Bondage-Breaking and Renunciation of Strongholds

1. I **confess** my sins (and my ancestor's sins) regarding the stronghold of
_____.

2. I **forgive** all who have influenced me to sin in this stronghold's area of
_____.

3. I **repent** of giving places to unclean spirits and strongholds in the area of
_____.

4. I **forgive myself** for the pain and limitations I have allowed this stronghold to inflict upon me, regarding _____.

5. In the name of Jesus, I **renounce and break** all agreements with the demonic stronghold of _____.

6. I **take authority** over the demonic stronghold of_____. I **command this stronghold** and anything associated with it to leave me now based on the finished work of Christ on the Cross and **my authority as a believer.**

7. I **praise You and thank You**, Father God, for protecting, healing, and delivering me. Thank You, Beloved Jesus, for dying for me. Thank You, Holy Spirit, for revealing this truth about the stronghold of _____ and **setting me free.** Hallelujah!

8. Holy Spirit, thank You for **exchanging the positive gift of** _____ for the negative stronghold of _____ as part of my divine redemption. Thank You, LORD, for making that exchange. I pray in Jesus's name. Amen.

Strongholds: 2 Corinthians 10:3-6
Confession: 1 John 1:9
Authority: Luke 10:19
Divine Exchange: Isaiah 53:4-6

Rebuking and Renouncing:
Any time Jesus cast out a demon, He *"ekballo"* (cast out) that demon.

What Can We Do About Suffering?

My experience with Paula is one reason I am writing this book. With the help and courage of Paula and others like her, I am learning the process of setting people free from darkness and suffering; I want to share this liberty. A few years ago, I would not have believed demons plagued my clients. But now, I have seen it with my own eyes. Seekers confirm they battle dark powers. A significant portion of mental health problems is caused by such demonic activity. The whispers about suicide, the hallucinations and delusions, and the self-cutting behaviors could have their origin in Satan's spiritual realm. The addictive cravings and the impulsive overdoses probably stem from evil.

Therefore, in our directive to help people with soul pain, we must educate ourselves regarding the ministry of deliverance. If this biblical paradigm seems right, decide how to proceed carefully. You will need your God-given authority that you received at the moment of belief in the eternal **salvation** of Jesus Christ. Belief in Jesus and your identity as a child of the King positions you to carry on these aspects of ministry.

[This authority is only for a believing Christian. It cannot be applied outside a genuine belief in Christ and His substitutionary death on the cross and subsequent resurrection.]

If this idea makes you apprehensive, remember that God's love frees us from fear. Recall the Lord's prayer: Even there we ask the heavenly Father to deliver us from evil. If you are a giver and are just learning about deliverance, please note that God wants you to take care of your own spiritual growth and make the necessary referrals to counselors trained in deliverance.

Suffering in this world is widespread. Our planet is the kingdom of darkness where Satan rules (temporarily) and men love darkness better than light.[181] Recently, I read these details in an email from Jay Sekulow, ACLJ[182] Chief Counsel:

> Christians are being exterminated: beheaded, enslaved, crucified…Syria's Christians–66 percent decimated. Iraq's Christians–82 percent destroyed or displaced. The numbers are staggering. The pain is unbearable.

How much of this evil is a direct result of demonic activity? I'd say all of it!

Frankly, the suffering we face in this safe cocoon of the United States is nothing compared to what is going on in other countries. My "sufferings" are *tiny* compared to the "suffering" of Christians who have been imprisoned and tortured, and have lost homes and loved ones. Regardless of our situation, we need to learn to live well with our *own* suffering. "To live well with" pain and suffering is more than tolerating it; it is courageously embracing the experience.

Consider Your Adversity a Blessing

To face suffering with courage, I suggest you consider your adversity as a blessing. I am *not* saying that adversity comes from God. (Absolutely not because there is no pain in the kingdom of God.) All painful difficulties have their origin in this fallen world. However, God says that He works pain into the fabric of our lives so that we can see His goodness in it. "And we know that in all things God works for the good of those who love him…."[183] This is how God redeems us—yes, frees us—from the curse of pain. Bob Sorge entitled his book on Job, *Pain, Perplexity and Promotion.*[184] The primary theme of his book is that the pain of suffering raises questions in our souls. As a result, our grappling

---

181 John 3:19

182 American Center for Law and Justice (ACLJ), www.aclj.org

183 Romans 8:28

184 Sorge, *Pain, Perplexity and Promotion.*

with that perplexity (about pain) promotes us to a greater intimacy with God.

Psychology has been practiced for more than 100 years. One of its goals has been to reduce humanity's suffering. I confess that my profession has made limited headway toward that goal. The reason why? Because the root of suffering cannot be explained within psychological constructs. We need to embrace its spiritual component. The origin of human suffering is fear, especially fear of death. Psychology has failed because it does not offer us a *lasting solution to fear*. Psychology cannot take the sting out of death. Death is a spiritual matter.

Whether we come at the problem of suffering from the point of view of mental health (science) or religion (faith), in both cases we face the problem of fear. Human beings are afraid of pain. Is there a solution for man's existential fear? Yes. Faith in Jesus has succeeded where psychology has failed. This is my experience and can be found as well in the testimonies of many people.

Jesus Is the Antidote to Fear and Suffering

How has **faith in Jesus** helped people overcome fear? Jesus undertook three actions, each of which gives us the victory over fear (see Figure 3 on page 208).

First, God said He would do just that—help us overcome fear. God does that by **giving us faith**. Jesus said, "…But take heart! I have overcome the world."[185] The Apostle John wrote: "…everyone born of God overcomes the world. This is the victory that has overcome the world, even our faith."[186]

Second, Jesus established **a covenantal promise**—the proclamation of God's Fatherhood. The One True God loves each

---

185 John 16:33

186 1 John 5:4

of us individually with a tender, personal devotion. Our Father in heaven promises provision and protection, despite the wicked forces surrounding us. The night before He was crucified, Jesus prayed to His Father, "My prayer is not that you take them out of the world but that you protect them from the evil one."[187] However, in order to benefit from this divine covenant, we have to comply with Holy God's challenging conditions. The heavenly Father assures us that He loves each one intimately and intensely. It is this love that propels us to choose obedience to the Almighty God. There—in that sweet spot of God's love—our fears are overcome. However, in that same spot, we are given a challenge. God calls us to choose between life and death.[188] Failure to obey the Lord—*even if stemming from ignorance or indifference*—is equivalent to disobedience. Our choice is this: Love and obey God, or default to the enemy's side. The former results in our receiving the heavenly Father's blessings, and the latter exposes us to Satan's curses.

The third action is **Jesus becoming the gate to peace** on earth. Fear is swallowed up when God's peace is present. The Apostle Paul wrote, "And the peace of God, which transcends all understanding, will guard your hearts and your minds in Christ Jesus."[189] Shalom peace is ours because Jesus took our deserved punishment onto Himself at the cross.[190] In other words, Jesus, knowing I was in an emotional mess, stepped up and said, "I'll pay her fine for that crime and do the jail time so that she can go free."

If you are having trouble comprehending this message about Jesus, don't despair. Here is a suggestion: Suspend your tendency to demand proof about this. Instead, embrace these ideas for 30 days as an act of faith, not one done by "sight" or scientific

---

187 John 17:15

188 Read Deuteronomy 30:15-20 for a more complete explanation.

189 Philippians 4:7

190 Isaiah 53:5

evidence. See what happens. I believe this choice will get you back to where you belong: *connected with God.*

Having **faith in Jesus is the reason we were created**. It's what the kingdom of God is all about. The Bible declares that there is no suffering in heaven: "He will wipe every tear from their eyes. There will be no more death or mourning, or crying or pain...."[191] When we reconnect with Father God, we are given solutions to our disbelief, our emotional problems, and our fears about pain and death.

Brother Alan Whittemore (my Uncle Pudge), wrote: "Fear itself is the very quintessence [embodiment] of pain. And Christ's proposal to us—the proposal of the Master both of religion and psychology—is to accept our pain for the love of the Father."[192] In his writings, Brother Whittemore challenged someone to pick up where he left off. Today, I am thrilled to write a psychology of suffering in response to my great uncle's request.

Readers, please extend grace to me, because I admit the psychology of suffering is a mystery. I don't fully understand what Uncle Pudge meant about "accepting our pain for the love of the Father." I believe that God's kingdom resources will flow down to earth at our request because Father God has opened the heavens to us. After all, the Father's will is that which is in heaven should be here on earth. That includes no pain or tears! Furthermore, I believe Jesus's blood has paid the price for our pain. "Surely our griefs [sicknesses] He Himself bore, and our sorrows [pain] He carried."[193] But, admittedly, I am perplexed. I still have days of pain in both my body and my heart. My life is one big learning curve, an ongoing adventure in diving into the depths of God.

---

191 Revelation 21:4

192 Alan G. Whittemore, *Joy in Holiness: A Collection of Letters and Other Writings of Spiritual Direction* (New York: Holy Cross Publications, 1964), 80-87.

193 Isaiah 53:4, New American Standard Bible

Figure 3

ANTIDOTE TO SOUL PAIN
Decision Tree: Make Choices for Freedom

OUTSIDE WORLD **TRIALS**

SOUL PAIN

INSIDE SELF **SUFFERING**

DAILY CHOOSE YOUR PATH

GOD'S WAY*
RESPOND IN FAITH
Be filled with the Holy Spirit.
Ephesians 5:18

INHALE
THE HOLY SPIRIT
Fruit of the Spirit is...
Galatians 5:22-23

FELLOWSHIP
WITH JESUS
"Remain in me..."
John 15:7

JOY
IN ALL TRIALS
[Jesus speaking:] "You will be filled with joy. Yes your joy will overflow!"
John 15:11 NLT

SPIRITUAL FREEDOM

STEPS TOWARD FREEDOM

BREAK THE LIE
"The Son sets you free."
John 8:36

CONFESS YOUR SIN
Confess our sins... and he will cleanse us.
1 John 1:9

MAN'S WAY*
RELIES ON SELF: SIN
For those who are self-seeking and who reject the truth... there will be wrath and anger.
Romans 2:8

FALL
INTO EVIL
There will be trouble and distress for every human being who does evil.
Romans 2:9

DISCONNECT
FROM GOD
This is how we know... who the children of the devil are: anyone who does not do what is right is not God's child.
1 John 3:10

IN BONDAGE
TO SATAN/DEMONS
[Opponents must]... escape from the trap of the devil, who has taken them captive to do his will.
2 Timothy 2:26

SPIRITUAL BONDAGE

Created by Julie Caton, Graphic Design by Laura Dudek

CONCLUSION

15

A Proposed Psychology
of Suffering

IN THE PROCESS of reflecting on this problem of suffering, I asked the Lord what He wanted to teach me. My learning labs on this lesson were my childhood rejections, academic difficulties, broken bones, difficult marriage, and the shame from the scam. The seasons of suffering I have shared are nothing compared to what other people have gone through, and no one's suffering could ever be compared to our Lord's.

But as a friend said to me, "Everybody's problem is the biggest because it is her own." It is out of these lessons that I share (with profound humility) what the Holy Spirit has taught me. May these ideas provide a "psychology of suffering" for any person struggling with soul pain. The Catholic priest, Henri Nouwen, wrote: "Pain is often what qualifies the counselor to lead others out of darkness and towards the light."[194] Those words describe my reasons for sharing ideas about suffering. May they help others to come into the light.

Practical Steps for Handling Suffering

I'd like to share a metaphor to unpack a process for managing suffering. My plan for getting through adversity is comparable to one that my friend, L.J., taught me about gardening. While these two experiences may seem polar opposites—suffering and gardening—they have a similar

---

194 Henri J.M. Nouwen, *The Wounded Healer* (Garden City: Doubleday, 1972).

blueprint in their "do"ing and a common goal. Both involve a progression to move the person to greater fruit. The gardener will see a harvest—of fruits and flowers. The seeker will experience a harvest—of enriched faith.

When I asked L.J. how she went about gardening, she laughed and said, "Well, of course, you have to *want to garden.* So, let me pause right there, and challenge you with this question:

Do you want to cultivate your faith so that you can bear spiritual fruit in the garden of suffering?

Just like L.J. had the deliberate intention of growing a garden, I have chosen to enlarge my worldview to allow for the presence of adversity. I'm learning how to live with it.

L.J. had to plan what type of garden she was creating because that **decision would affect the spot** she would choose to break ground. For me, to "break ground" spiritually speaking, I must accept the fact that suffering will happen. We exist in a fallen world with an antagonist (the enemy of our souls) who provokes suffering.[195] Because of that reality, I need to cultivate this special "garden bed": a daily mindset in which my soul readies itself for the next season of suffering and pain. As long as I am alive on earth, suffering will come. Yet, it will not master me.

"When you pick the spot for your garden," L.J. told me, "you need to be sure there will be a lot of sun because that is the main ingredient for growth." In this metaphor, I need the Son to nourish my spiritual seeds. Thus, I study Jesus's life and teachings, which grow my faith, so when suffering comes, **I believe it will transform me.**[196] Because I'm willing to be changed, I can **embrace** my suffering, even give thanks for it!

Suffering can be the portal through which we deepen our relationship with the Creator. How might that happen? Consider

195 John 10:10

196 2 Corinthians 3:18

this: When we pray for healing due to sickness, but healing does not come at that time—unanswered prayers cause continued suffering. So how can this experience bring positive transformation?

Because God's "no, not yet" kindles my faith.[197]

Such circumstances challenge me to **walk by faith.** I acknowledge that I am living in this world temporarily with my feet firmly planted on the earth, but I am *not of this world.*[198] I tap into the supernatural power of the kingdom of God while here on earth and activate faith. I intentionally keep my eyes on Jesus and not on the events threatening me with pain. Because God tells me faith in Him is more valuable than gold,[199] I keep banking the gold that accumulates through these acts of the faith.

In the beginning when L.J. designed a garden bed, she worked hard to break up the clods and to stir up the soil. In this spiritual metaphor, my soul must break up unplowed ground when God doesn't answer prayer the way that I wish He would. Because of the hardened soil, I must push deeper into Him, asking Him for stronger faith. This digging deep shapes and strengthens my character, and enriches my relationship with God.

Which do you believe is more valuable: *my basic intimacy with God or my experience of God-given healing?* I believe the more important outcome is building divine relationship with God because that is what will last for eternity. Once I'm in heaven, whatever healing I experienced on earth is a moot point.

During her seasons of gardening, L.J. consulted experts and books. Likewise, in the process of tending my "garden" and embracing suffering, I set my eyes on Jesus, my Master Gardener. He is the suffering servant[200] who overcame death through His

---

197 2 Corinthians 5:7

198 John 15:19

199 1 Peter 1:7

200 Isaiah 53:3

crucifixion and resurrection. He is my mentor. When I **turn and gaze upon the Resurrected Christ**, I achieve victory over my fears[201] because Jesus ended the fear of death.

L.J. explained that a gardener needs to plan for different seasons. She had her time of preparation, then planting, maintenance, and finally harvest. Even then, the year isn't over yet; she planned for the winter months when her perennials will lay dormant, pushing their roots deep into the soil as they prepare for rebirth in the spring.

I, too, compartmentalize my life into several seasons:

- **Before** a time of suffering, I anticipate the inevitable: *There will be suffering.*[202] I am intentional about building this worldview: God and I are *partnering* through the adversity of life. I am not alone. I read my Bible, worship God, and pray to establish greater intimacy with Immanuel, *God with us.*

- **During** the difficult time in which I am cultivating my faith, I work the soil of my soul to remove rocks, roots, and weeds. I spot the burgeoning flowers or vegetables, and clear the way for their full growth.

- **In the midst of the harvest**, I pick the flowers and the fruit, and rejoice in the fulfillment of my intention. This spiritual fruit will remain forever.[203]

- **After** the adversity, I plan for the future. For a short time, there is a period of dormancy and preparation for the next cycle.

To learn how these practical steps help me to persevere through suffering, continue reading for a deeper look at the process.

---

201 Hebrews 12:2

202 2 Timothy 3:12; 1 Peter 4:12; and James 1:2

203 John 15:16

The Planting Season

Before I'm in a season of suffering, I sow the seeds of <u>good spiritual habits</u>.

One such habit is the practice of **"dying to self" daily.**[204] This is equivalent to breaking up the soil and **planting the seed.** Just like the seed has to be buried in the soil and die in order to germinate, likewise, I "die to self." Simply put, this term means I give up my rights to an expectation that "everything must go well." Each little problem reminds me that life is not pain-free and not always comfortable.

Continuing with the gardening metaphor, another habit is to stir fertilizer into the soil around each seed. This "plant food" is my maintaining an attitude of thanksgiving. I love the way the Huron Indians farmed 300 years ago. After breaking up their hardened ground, they would till a straight furrow and place their seeds in it along with dead fish. As the fish decayed, it fertilized the corn, squash, and beans.[205] In practical terms, the process of fertilizing the seed (which is "dying to self") is **giving thanks to God for the adversity.** This simple act of gratitude disarms Satan and steals his power. When God acts in these small details of my life, offering up a sacrifice of thanksgiving[206] is a rewarding (although somewhat painful) experience.

Tending the Garden

In the **middle phase**, as the garden grows, L.J. said that the activity she liked the least was the one that was the most important: **weeding.** She had to keep up with it, or the "bad" plants would overrun the "good" plants. She did not want them robbing her baby plants of the nutrients they each needed in order to mature.

---

204 Luke 9:23-24

205 For more information on the Native American way of life in the 18th Century, refer to my historical novel, *White Heart.*

206 Hebrews 13:15

For me, the weeds and thistles in the garden of my soul are the "worries of this world, the deceitfulness of riches, and the desires for other things which choke out the word in my heart making it unfruitful."[207]

My action step (of weeding) is this: **I confirm my intention to walk in obedience**[208] to Jesus and to stay filled with the Holy Spirit. He is my weed-whacker, and I turn Him loose on the weeds. I ask Him to remove anything that is not "good." I make sure the "voices" that are filling my head (e.g., what I listen to on media, conversations I have with people, or even self-talk) are positive and pure, carrying only God-given messages—not defeating thoughts.

As the garden matures and progresses toward harvest time, there is much work to be done. Each day, L.J. had to exert herself to do pest control, trim dead flowers, cut back gangly branches, and make sure the plants had plenty of water.

During my spiritual season of pain, I tend my [soul] "garden" daily, particularly making sure it has plenty of water (the Holy Spirit). God freely offers me what I need, but I am responsible to rise up, move out, pull the weeds, apply the pesticide, connect the hose, and yes—even turn on the spigot! This takes active discipline, or the soul garden will not thrive. God invites us to call on His Holy Spirit, but we must turn the hose on and keep it gushing. Gardening—either actual plants or spiritual habits—takes work!

Spiritually speaking, the equivalent to pulling weeds is this: **I let my feelings out.** I weep. I scream if needed. I acknowledge the reality of the pain. I might write a poem, paint a picture, smash a cheap vase, or scribble in a journal. I run. I dig. I swim. I box. I pull real weeds.

---

207 Mark 4:19

208 John 14:21

These "weeds" that hinder the growth of my faith usually take the form of fear in some way. So, **I have to shake off any residue of fear.** When my gut feels fear, or threatening thoughts pop into my head, I acknowledge them, but I don't belabor them. I label them because I know the truth sets me free.[209] Once identified, I can place those toxic feelings at the *foot of the cross* and ask Jesus to get rid of them.[210]

The feeling of **fear has three root causes**: cellular damage, ungodly beliefs, and dark energy called the "spirit of fear":

1. The first cause of fear, **cellular damage**, is the fact my body's cells remember events from my past, causing me fear. For me to get over it, the cells' molecular reaction needs to be normalized, a process including relaxation, the healing of memories, and inner healing. I ask the Holy Spirit to help heal these injuries.

2. The second trigger of fear comes from **ungodly beliefs**, or the untruths planted by the father of lies.[211] If I hold on to ungodly beliefs, I am empowering the devil's lies. So, I find biblical truths that contradict Satan's lies, and I declare them out loud. My first declaration is claiming the weapon that annihilated the devil, which is the *spilled blood* of Jesus.[212] Then, I *take authority over the enemy* and his deceptive tactics.[213]

3. The third cause of fear is a simple one: For some reason, **a dark, spiritual entity has landed** on me, like a spider dropping on my shoulder in a dirty old barn. God tells us, "I have not given you a spirit of fear."[214] This suggests there are spirits of fear sneaking around,

209 John 8:32

210 1 John 1:9

211 John 8:44

212 Revelation 12:11

213 Luke 10:19

214 2 Timothy 1:7

intent on destroying the peace and joy in my life. In this situation, God gives me the authority in Christ *to rebuke* (i.e., terminate his influence) this spirit of fear. Once it is sent away, I quickly replace the void it left by asking the Holy Spirit to fill me with God's love, power, and good judgment.

Often, I have to wrestle with God and that vile spirit of fear. Frequently, the spirit I am battling is "fear of the unknown." When I am in the midst of fear, I remember to position myself securely in Jesus. I speak God's protection against evil over my life. During these wrestling matches, you'll find me reading sections of Scripture aloud and declaring victory, even though I don't feel it in the moment. Despite the fact that I feel embarrassed because I'm troubled, I contact praying friends and ask them to intercede. This stage is not a quick or quiet process.

At some point, the battle tips in my favor. Finally, when all that plagued me in the state of "unknown" disappears, I experience God's presence. Once I am *in step with God*, I settle into His unconditional love. When that happens, His perfect love throws my fear to the curb.[215]

During my experiences with physical and emotional pain, I have discovered that I manage pain more easily than fear. Pain is a defined target, centralized and identifiable. It wanes as time passes. If it is physical pain, I can put ice on it or take an aspirin. If it is emotional pain, I can cry or scream.

Fear, on the other hand, is an emotional heaviness from which I can't wiggle away. One has to find the will to stand and walk through it because fear fades only when one is brave enough to move into it. In my own power, I do not have the courage to step out afraid, but through the Holy Spirit's strength within me, I

---

215 1 John 4:18

can face that fear. As Scripture says, "If God is for us, who can be against us?"[216]

The Harvest

In this metaphor, **the harvested** fruit is Victory Over Suffering. This fruit ripens slowly over time. I keep working "the garden." **I study Jesus.** This has a two-fold benefit. First, Jesus is my model for handling pain. I can watch how He does it. Second, Jesus took the lashes for me. This is a promise from God: "Surely he took up our pain and bore our suffering...."[217] During painful periods, I visualize Jesus's face or His body on the cross and breathe deeply into that reality. The Apostle Paul writes that we are to take our thoughts captive to the Lord Jesus Christ.[218] The verb "to take captive" has the word picture of a conquering soldier (me) holding her spear (the Word) toward the back of my enemy (my fear or pain) and walking it into a prison cell.

I call out to the Comforter (Holy Spirit). I push through, fighting against the temptation to be numb and disconnected. I say words like: "Fill me with Your love. Activate Your love now! Let me love You, *and* let me feel You loving me. I am not alone. Your love will cast out my fear. Let it be so!" I believe God has a plan for me, even when I don't understand it all. I argue if I'm angry. I complain if I'm weary. I question if I'm confused.

I praise the Lord. Sometimes, this praising is done through gritted teeth, devoid of any pleasant feeling. When I speak out loud my praise to the Lord, I am being obedient. We are asked to provide the sacrifice of praise from our lips.[219] Also, I am

---

216 Romans 8:31

217 Isaiah 53:4

218 2 Corinthian 10:5

219 Hebrews 13:15

silencing the enemy because Scripture says that spoken praise turns the foe on his heel.[220]

Dormancy

By **the winter season,** the harvest has come and gone. The season of suffering has passed, and the battle has quieted down. During this time, I try to take several restorative actions while adversity appears to be dormant.

Just as gardeners welcome the snows of winter and the showers of April, water in the ground continues to be a necessity. So, **I run to the well** of the Holy Spirit and fill myself up again by seeking out corporate worship with other Christian believers.

I welcome opportunities for intercession: praying for others and also asking others to pray for me. This activity helps me to recall past harvests. **I seek opportunities to participate in miracles,** which come in the form of blessings and healing prayer for others.

In truth, this dormant season is power-packed. During this time, I **devour the Word** and ask God to teach me more about **how I can participate in the kingdom of God** in preparation for the next harvest.

Throughout all of this, **I also care for my body,** which may have worn out a bit from all my "gardening." It needs pastoring, which includes rest, refreshment, and recreation.

And the cycle repeats itself.

The Holy Spirit unpacked this verse for me:

For who has despised the day of small things? But these seven [spirits of God] will be glad when they see the plumb line in the hand of

---

220 Psalm 8:2, New English Translation: "…you have ordained praise on account of your adversaries, so that you might put an end to the vindictive enemy."

Zerubbabel—*these are* the eyes of the Lord which range to and fro throughout the earth.[221]

My personal paraphrase of this verse is:

Embrace and enjoy the small things that happen to you. It is in the small things where God sees you as you build yourself with a straight plumb line. The Spirit of the Lord is watching you and rejoicing as you align with His plan.

While I don't have all the answers as to why these "little things" happen and cause me pain and frustration, I believe that they help me cultivate a deeper relationship with the Lord. For that reason alone, I can give thanks in all circumstances.[222]

A New Paradigm—Jesus as Our Model

I am proposing a **new paradigm**: It is radically new in the field of mental health, but ancient in other ways because it is based on Jesus's life, death, and resurrection. **Jesus alone should be at the heart of our response to mental health problems.** The revolutionary teachings and ministry of Jesus declare the antidote to pain and fear. By connecting with Jesus, we learn a psychology of suffering applicable in any situation.

Why is Jesus's paradigm radical? Because **Jesus's teachings are different from the world's ideas.** This God-man, the carpenter from Nazareth, states that **man is sinful,** and yet **God loves each of us** anyway, even while He grieves over our tendency to go our own independent way. Jesus suggests that we shouldn't continue to believe that we are "good." Instead, we should acknowledge that we were created originally as "good," *but* our rebellious spirits and pride caused us to disobey God. Only through Christ's righteousness are we restored to "good" in God's eyes.

---

221 Zechariah 4:10, New American Standard Bible

222 1 Thessalonians 5:18

If we are going to embrace this paradigm, we must stop thinking that our independence from God is healthy. The truth is just the opposite: **We were created to be dependent on God.** Because we have challenged God and have chosen to do things our own way, we have broken off this ideal relationship with the Creator; this original design was God's best for us. Our separation from God has left us feeling naked and unprotected, the source of anxiety and stress. **Mankind's disconnection from God is the cause of mental illness.** We live in a world that has been corrupted, and sin is the current of our river. We must understand that we are caught in its flow and become aware of our options.

Many do not believe this statement: **There is an enemy of our souls** who is alive and well on planet Earth. Our enemy goes to great lengths to hide this truth, while he is actively seeking to throw pain and suffering at us. The great news is that Satan has been destroyed through Jesus's death and resurrection. But most of us don't know this. Those of us who know it, don't believe it on a practical level. Jesus, who has **defeated this enemy,** is the fundamental **solution to mental illness.** In most counseling sessions, Jesus's victory over illness is not discussed, but it should be, since the **Son of God** died for us, ultimately helping with our mental health!

The idea of our good God sacrificing His Son by crucifixion is difficult to understand. The best explanation is found in the historical event of the Passover,[223] the season during which God freed His people from slavery in Egypt. God instructed Moses to have the Hebrew people sprinkle the blood of lambs on the doorposts of their homes. This blood protected them from the unleashed spirit of destruction, whose mission was to kill all the firstborn not covered in the lamb's blood. The Passover is the great event when the blood of a lamb set the Hebrew people free and protected them from evil. I cannot

---

223 Exodus 12

explain how it works, but based on Scripture and faith, I declare it is true.

Jesus is our human model in this paradigm. While on earth, He showed us how to live free from the influence of the enemy. He taught us how to follow in His godly footsteps. He demonstrated healthy principles for living. Finally, He presented the "how-to" for one's salvation, healing, and deliverance.

After He was crucified, Jesus overcame death, entered heaven, and released the Holy Spirit to believers. **Mental illness is treated most effectively when this power source of the Holy Spirit is unleashed.** When you were born physically, God gave you His breath of life. But spiritual transformation within you comes only when you **ask for His Holy Spirit**. Think of the Holy Spirit as a key; its keyhole is in the door to your heart. You want to take the key (Holy Spirit) and open that door (your spirit) and invite Jesus to come into you. At that moment, God replaces your "self" with God's presence, and change takes place. You become a whole new person.[224] You are born again and reconnected with the Creator—the sweet spot where we were meant to be in the first place!

The **Holy Spirit offers three treasures** to help with suffering. First, He brings Godly comfort. Because of the Holy Spirit's presence, our fears—of the unknown, pain, and death—no longer threaten us because they are swallowed up by God's love. In the midst of any adversity, God's Spirit offers us joy and solace. Also, He brings wise counsel, removing offenses and guilt, so that our emotional problems are more likely to heal. Finally, His very name (which in Greek is *parakletos*) means the Advocate, or Redeemer. In other words, "He has erased the curse of evil" from us.

Jesus wants us—as givers—to offer full healing and deliverance to any wounded soul. Jesus calls us—as seekers—to His outstretched arms. His embrace wraps us in divine love and

---

224 2 Corinthians 5:17

supernatural peace. In either role, Jesus offers us a way to build a relationship with Him.

Let's Get Practical

Permit me to shift my message from these heavenly doctrines and spiritual truths back down to earth—to the chairs in the counseling office. You might be a mental health counselor or a pastor or lay minister. You might be a wounded soul, seeking help. Either way, here we sit, face-to-face, looking for *more*, so a life can be revitalized. Whether we are in the role of giver or seeker, or both, let's get really practical. Where do we start?

Bring Almighty God into the relationship. Our foundational position is this: Father God, who created us, loves us immensely. Think of God as a deep well and the water in that well as the nutrient needed to change soul pain and nurture ourselves. First, I suggest that we start by dipping our bucket into that well of divine power.

However, the very act of believing that there is a well into which we can lower the bucket takes trust. So, here is the second step: The seeker may need to develop trust with the human giver first before he is prepared to trust God. One's human therapeutic relationship may be the beginning of one's eternal partnership with God.

Let's say that drinking from this bucket is the equivalent to shoring up who you are in Christ. Whether you are a giver or a seeker, the **second, practical step of healing is to strengthen one's identity**.

Once we have drunk our fill (i.e., established who we are in Christ), God's love will flow through us. This love will enable greater trust between giver and seeker, and seeker and God. Then, we can choose the best way—tools and principles uniquely designed for this situation by the Creator—to achieve health and wholeness. You are now free to reconsider your worldview and make a life-changing shift in the direction of greater health. All of this takes time and perseverance.

Because you have developed a clearer picture of who you are, you are no longer frightened to try something different. A vulnerable **partnership of trust** has been established. Love is exchanged. With that refreshed or newly formed identity, you are free to **"rethink" yourself**. No longer afraid of a shattered sense of self, you can alter your paradigm. And healing happens. This process of **changing your perspective is the third practical step** to health.

Earlier in the book, you were introduced to Jesus's suggestion that we "repent" or "rethink" our situation. The Christian author, Ted Dekker, highlights this critical process in many of his writings. Born to and raised by missionaries who lived among a cannibalistic tribe, Dekker has become a best-selling author. To illustrate the importance of "rethinking" ourselves and "repenting" of our old paradigm, the following is excerpted from his novel, *The 49th Mystic*.

During one of the crises in the story, two of the lead characters were on their way to managing a major conflict. This is the conversation that took place between the spiritually mature "savior figure," Talya, and the young heroine, Rachelle, who is forming her newfound identity as a spiritually empowered mystic.

"I don't see how [I can walk on water]," [Rachelle says].

"The idea that you can't is only a story you've been led to believe, no more real than any other tall tale you've bound yourself to, thus making it so in your experience. Try it." [Talya says].

"But I..."

Talya stepped off the shore and walked into the lake. But then I saw that his feet weren't in the water. They were *on* it, as if the surface was made of soft glass. I blinked and looked closer, stunned by the slight bending of the water under his sandals.

He turned, faced me with a mischievous glint in his eyes, and spread his arms. "This...is the story I believe."

I gawked at him. "How?"

"**Through a shift in perception, our entire lives change**. It's the **basis for all that is miraculous**—the shifting of our perception of the material world beyond time and space. When you look at what's beneath me, what do you see?"

"Water," I said.

"And can you walk on it?"

I looked at the shimmering water under his feet. "No."

"And so you are bound by that belief. Instead, look with new eyes. Change your cognitive perception, your thinking. Yeshua called this practice *metanoia* as written in ancient Greek. *Meta,* which means 'change' or 'beyond' and *noia,* meaning 'thinking' or 'knowing'. Metanoia."

He made it sound so simple, but nothing about him standing there in that impossible place seemed simple to me. "Just rewire my mind?"

"Don't conform to the patterns of the world you see. **Step off the shore of your old mind and into a new mind.** Walk on water."

"I don't see how I can do that," Rachelle said.

"Try it and you will see how....**Have no fear**, we only just begin."[225]

If I can ask one thing of you, it is to rethink your worldview. Review the truth that you are not just a body, or even just a body connected to a soul. Consider this: You have a spirit that is created to be connected with God's spirit. In that partnership, you will find new solutions to dealing with mental illness—yours or that of others.

Throughout reading *Soul Pain Revealed,* you have met many seekers. You've learned about various interventions that givers use. You've read the highlighted truth about mankind's troubled nature, our negative emotions, the consequences of mental imbalances, and potential seasons of suffering. Here, we have seen this reality: The **loving Creator has a plan to help us**

---

225 Ted Dekker, *The 49th Mystic: Beyond the Circle* (Grand Rapids: Revell, 2018), 166-167.

through our suffering. The door into that reality may simply start with a loving, trusting relationship with a giver.

Certainly, we may use medication and clinical therapy along the way. We may need psychiatric hospitalization or psychological assessments, too. Hopefully, one's foundational therapeutic relationship will open up a spiritual treasure chest that will bring healing. Each of us needs to decide if the biblical truths presented seem right for us. As we bridge psychological principles with faith-based beliefs, I hope we each find our way through suffering. In order to achieve mental health and to experience the love of God, I urge you to not be afraid. Go ahead and change your way of thinking.

Let me close this book with a prayer for you and a letter to address your heart.

A CLOSING PRAYER

D EAR FATHER GOD,

We thank You for creating us. Thank You for giving us the breath of life, the choice, and the means to connect with You. Please forgive our instinct to go it alone. By operating independently from You, we cause our own pain, fear, and difficulties.

Give us the heart of a dependent child, secure in Your love, Heavenly Father. Help us to trust You wholeheartedly. Please heal the wounds in our souls.

We ask You to equip us with two things so that we can be mentally healthy: *sound minds* and *compassionate hearts*. Fill us with Your Holy Spirit, so we can bring healing to the people around us who have soul pain, ourselves included. Give us boldness to embrace this paradigm and to spread the message: *Jesus offers spiritual freedom* and emotional health to all who will receive it.

We declare complete healing for all of the people You have placed in our lives. Just like Jesus did, we will use our God-given authority and the power of His name and identity to complete this mission. We offer ourselves as chalices to You. Please fill us with the wine of Your Spirit so that we can offer healing and health to others.

Father, Son, and Holy Spirit—You have shown us how mental *health* can abound in our world. Make it so, Lord.

We ask these things in the mighty name of Jesus. Amen.

EPILOGUE:
THE QUESTION OF ETERNITY

DEAR FRIEND,

In this last season, the Lord has prompted me to write the following letter. I offer it to you out of my love, as I want to be sure you have a chance to consider what I believe to be the most important question of all: **What are you doing about God and eternity?**

If you are reading this letter, we have a mutual concern about mental health. You may have come to me because there is an emotional or family issue in your life. You may have read this book, Soul Pain Revealed. *Or you may be tired of the "messes" going on around you. Be assured: I want to help you with that.*

But **I believe there is an even bigger concern that should be our focus.** *This is the message that describes a way of life dear to my heart—your* **partnering with God.** *Perhaps you may be too focused on your mess and can't see a way out. Maybe you crave more love, more peace, and more hope, but you are not yet experiencing it.*

Stick with me because I think what **you really yearn for is what I've found.** *I messed up my life as a young person and had to have a change of heart. God made it possible by helping me to "rethink" life. God helped me to put my past behind me, giving me a hope and a future. When I felt like a failure as a high school student, Jesus entered my life. Later, when I became a psychologist and experienced difficulties in my marriage, Jesus helped me through those tough times.*

Most of us **feel we're incomplete,** *or that something is missing, but we are not sure what. Most of us weren't raised in a* *family that took God seriously. Perhaps our grandparents respected religion and church, but few family members focused on how to develop a personal relationship with God. Yet, did you know that you were conceived with this **life's purpose: to be in partnership with the Creator?***

You may be living a life disconnected from God. Your choice may have just snuck up on you because no one has told you that knowing God is important. Probably you didn't intend to ignore God. I'm guessing that you hadn't planned on breaking any of God's rules, but oops!

*I will remind you while you are alive on this planet that you really are connected with the Creator whether you like it or not; it is His breath that you breathe. But there's much more that you might want to know about our worldly existence. For one, **there is an enemy of our souls,** whom the Bible calls the devil. That enemy tries to dupe us into believing that we are okay without God. Possibly you feel that way, too—that you are okay without God.*

But you are mistaken.

*I share this, not as a judgment, but as **a wake-up call.** Without an active relationship with God, your life is incomplete. If you continue down this path, you may die without God in your life. Your soul will continue existing for eternity—but in the absence of God. It's your choice whether or not you will experience God's love, peace, and promise of heaven.*

The devil wants you to believe these ideas: You are complete unto yourself and don't need God in your life. And it's okay that your soul just drops into a godless eternity, which Satan declares is a manmade myth, so no big deal.

Hey! The devil is a liar! And, if you are not with God, you are unintentionally against God and in the devil's space. Within that darkness, there is judgment and fear, betrayal and corruption, immorality and despair.

While your life's problems are annoying—and hopefully we can overcome them—the more important question is this:

What are you doing about God and eternity?

I know it's hard to think about eternity. After all, the **kingdom of God is invisible.** *We don't see it, much less feel it. However, the Bible makes it clear that we are surrounded by distinct, invisible, spiritual realms. Within one, you partner with the prince of lies and his foul darkness. Within the other, you join with God and experience divine* **love and light, health and hope.**

Plus, the Bible says that our souls live on for eternity.

The choice is yours: *Are you heading to heaven (i.e., with God) or to hell (i.e., without God)?*

Now, because of this letter, you are aware of your position and can't therefore say, "Well, I didn't know." Some people have been deeply wounded by the church or authority figures, while others are clearly rebellious toward God. But many others—and this is more likely you if you are a "good" person who hasn't given control to God—are simply **indifferent to spiritual matters.** *Whether you are actively working against God, running from Him, or passively ignoring all things about Him, somehow you have turned a blind eye to the consequences of eternity.*

We all need Jesus in our lives. Why? Because our imperfections block us from knowing God and experiencing the love of the Almighty in its fullness. His shed blood erases these sins. You have read that **Jesus, the Son of God, is the pathway to knowing our Almighty Creator** *(see Figure 4 on page 235). Through Jesus, the heavenly Father reached down to end our self-absorption and to enter our lives by giving us His Holy Spirit.*

If you have surrendered control of your life to Him, the Spirit of God has entered you. He is the key that has unlocked the door to your heart—because of your invitation. If that is so, the Holy Spirit is transforming you into a godly person, a Christ-one. Be sure of this: **Our Loving God has a plan for you**—*a plan to prosper you and give you peace and hope.*

*But, if you have not surrendered control, you are forfeiting a place with God, and, by omission, you are on the enemy's team. The enemy, a.k.a. **the devil, has a plan for you,** but not a nice plan. He wants to kill, steal, and destroy all that is good in your life.*

*Our heavenly Father does not want that defeated life for you. Father God and I yearn for you to live a rich, fulfilled life, which you can do once you are part of the kingdom of God. So, dear friend, please take two minutes. **Decide to surrender to God,** so that you can **live with Him for eternity.** My heart breaks with the thought of your suffering and existing forever without God, in the realm of the devil. All you have to say is:*

Dear Jesus,

Please forgive my pride. I need You. Thank You for dying for my sins. I give You control of my life. I invite You into my heart. Today, from this very minute forward and for eternity, I will live for You.

I pray this in the name of Jesus. Amen.

*Contact me at drjuliecaton@gmail.com if you have made this decision and want to know the next step. This is just the beginning. **It is a lifestyle choice.** I love you.*

Signed,
Dr. Julie

But seek first his kingdom and his righteousness, and all these things will be given to you as well.
(Matthew 6:33)

Figure 4

BIBLICAL OVERVIEW OF SUFFERING

Diagram outlines the interaction between God and man regarding suffering and its solution. The outer circle is a description of God's Action, and the inner circle is Man's Response.

GOD'S ORDAINED DESTINY FOR MAN

BEGINNING

FALL OF HUMANITY: EVIL RULES EARTH

JESUS BRIDGES HUMANITY + GOD

LIVING THE SPIRIT-FILLED LIFE

God created all creation to live in harmony to be God's glory.

Out of love, God gave man free will.

God provides temporary solutions to man's suffering through old covenant.

Man + Woman thrive sin-free in the Garden as the Glory of God.

Man chooses to live independently of God.

Man is separated from God, causing fear and suffering.

Patriarchs & Prophets carry message of God's love/redemption.

Sin, corruption, disease and death plague mankind.

Man is restored physically, emotionally and spiritually & finds his way through suffering.

Humanity is introduced to God-in-the-flesh, i.e, the incarnation of Jesus .

Jesus experiences fullness of being God while enduring suffering of being human.

By this God-centered choice, man is empowered to be restored.

Man is given choice to partner with Holy Spirit and be transformed into the image of God.

Man is given the choice to receive Jesus as Redeemer.

Jesus is crucified to pay for man's sin. His death defeats Evil.

God fully restores humanity: body-soul-spirit; God provides answer to man's suffering.

Holy Spirit gives daily restoration.

Holy Spirit is released to mankind because the Crucified Jesus is resurrected.

Created and designed by Laura Dudek

Appendix A
Glossary of Mental Health Terms

Anxiety
A description of a mental state characterized by excessive agitation, both physically (i.e., rapid heart and breathing) and/or mentally (i.e., uncontrollable and swirling thought patterns). The person struggles with constant worrying, whether or not there is a reason for the fear. An **anxiety attack or panic attack** is the event in which the person is overwhelmed by a groundless fear and extreme agitation that derails his normal functioning.

Attention Deficit Hyperactivity Disorder (ADHD)
A neurodevelopmental disorder defined by difficulties with attention, mental disorganization, and/or hyperactivity-impulsivity. Other characteristics include lack of persistence, low frustration tolerance, intolerance of boredom, and mood swings. These problems need to occur in at least three settings (school, home, and social situations) in order to confirm the diagnosis.[226]

Autism Spectrum Disorder (ASD)
A description of a person who has persistent deficits in social communication and interaction. This leads to trouble with developing and maintaining social relationships. People with Autism Spectrum Disorder often exhibit repetitive behavior patterns that are inflexible, repetitive, and out of the norm.[227] In 2013, the diagnosis of **Asperger's Syndrome** was reclassified as a subset of ASD. The distinguishing traits of someone formerly described as having Asperger's are the following: the person may

---

226 *Diagnostic and Statistical Manual of Mental Disorders*, 57.

227 Ibid., 50.

be smart regarding book knowledge but immature regarding social interactions because of trouble with obsessive thinking and chronic social anxiety. Often, someone with Asperger's is described as a person on the "high functioning end" of the Autism Spectrum.[228]

Bipolar Disorder

A mental health disorder characterized by the person having periods of distinct moods, changing rapidly within hours, or over weeks and months. The moods range from manic to depressive, and include irritability, sleep disturbance, and changes in speech patterns.[229]

Brain Anatomy

In the human being, the brain is a large mass of nerve tissue enclosed in the skull, comprising two cerebral hemispheres. It is regarded as the seat of consciousness. See Chapter Four's *Psych 101: Medication and Brain Anatomy* for further explanation.

Defense Mechanism

A defense mechanism is an unconscious strategy a person uses to help deal with the painful emotions within his soul. The strategy could be a way of thinking (e.g., **denial**, "No I don't do that," when in fact he does), **negative humor** like sarcasm, or **projection** (e.g., misperceiving the motives of another person when the motives are actually coming from within you). These are just a few. Google *defense mechanisms* for a comprehensive list. All of us use defense mechanisms; some have more serious psychological consequences than others.

Depression

A description of a mental state when a person is chronically sad, unmotivated, often feels hopeless and helpless, and is overwhelmed by emotions of guilt and shame. **Depressive Disorder** is the professional, diagnostic term for a person

---

228 "Autism Spectrum Disorders (ASD) Center: Symptoms, Causes, Tests, Treatment, and Therapies," WebMD, accessed May 22, 2019, http://www.webmd.com/brain/autism.

229 *Diagnostic and Statistical Manual of Mental Disorders,* 123-168.

struggling with depression, and describes someone who is failing to function normally because of depression. **Seasonal Affective Disorder** is one form of depression brought on by less daylight, colder temperatures, and reduced exposure to the sun and outdoors.

Eating Disorder

Eating disorders are characterized by a persistent disturbance of eating-related behavior. This results in the person having altered eating habits that impair her physical and mental health. The most common ones are **anorexia nervosa** (in which the person restricts calories and fears weight gain) and **bulimia nervosa** (in which a person binge-eats and then uses behaviors like vomiting to prevent weight gain).[230]

Erik Erikson's Psychosocial Stages of Development

Erikson was a student of Sigmund Freud's daughter, Anna, and used Freud's theory of personality as the foundation for his psychosocial stages of development. The psychosocial approach looks at individuals in the context of the combined influences of their psychological traits and their social environment and how these each impact their physical and mental wellness.[231] Around 1953, Erikson coined the term "identity crisis," stating that resolving that crisis is the task of adolescent development. "**Identity** is a term that reflects the inner continuity between what one was as a child and what one is becoming as an adult."[232]

---

230 Ibid., 329-354.

231 "Psychosocial," Wikipedia, March 07, 2019, accessed May 22, 2019, https://en.wikipedia.org/wiki/Psychosocial.

232 Erikson, *A Way of Looking at Things*, 634.

Information Substances
The 1990s term used for the chemicals responsible for emotions within our body, based on the research done by Candace Pert, M.D. (1946-2013).[233]

Mania
Behavior characterized by excessive emotion and thoughts as well as disordered speech and thinking so that the person is acting "crazy" (to varying degrees). A **manic episode** is the period of time the person demonstrates this excessive energy and rambling speech pattern. He may set and pursue goals that are unrealistic and potentially dangerous.

Mental Disorder
A mental disorder is a "syndrome characterized by clinically significant disturbances in the individual's cognition, emotional regulation, and/or behavior that reflect inability to function in his psychological, biological, and developmental processes."[234]
One's **capacity to function** refers to the natural and characteristic action of somebody with respect to areas of daily living, working, and relating to other people.

Mental Post-Mortem
Just as a corpse may undergo an autopsy so that the physician can better understand the cause of death, so do mental health professionals examine (after a suicide) the psychological make-up of a person who dies by his own hand. This increases our understanding of the risk factors and underlying causes of suicide in general. We ask ourselves, "What did we overlook?"

Overmedication
The condition of a person who has consumed pills for a mental health problem, causing him to have an adverse reaction. The overmedicated person may feel "not himself"; his thoughts may

---

233 Pert, *Molecules of Emotion*, 141; John Schwartz, "Candace Pert, 67, Explorer of the Brain, Dies," *The New York Times*, September 19, 2013, accessed May 23, 2019, https://www.nytimes.com/2013/09/20/science/candace-pert-67-explorer-of-the-brain-dies.html.
234 *Diagnostic and Statistical Manual of Mental Disorders*, 20.

race, or he may be excessively upset or tired, and just plain "out of it." Overmedicating oneself can lead to an unintentional suicide attempt.

Personality Disorder

A person with a personality disorder has a chronic pattern of both internal experience and external behavior distinctly different from that of his culture or of those in the environment around him. The personality disorder may cause him distress throughout his life. The common characteristics are inflexibility in certain areas, such as suspicious thinking, entitled behavior, preoccupation with control, and pervasive trouble in relationships. Based on research, a person with a personality disorder usually struggles with an unstable or nonexistent personal identity. Types of personality disorders include **Borderline, Antisocial, Dependent,** to name a few.[235]

Post-Traumatic Stress Disorder (PTSD)

This disorder is characterized by four criteria:

1. The person must have experienced a trauma in which he *felt* like his life was being threatened.
2. His trauma memory has caused high levels of agitation, anxiety, and/or anger.
3. He tries to cope with the problem by numbing himself emotionally and avoiding anything that stirs up the trauma.
4. He experiences nightmares or flashbacks of the event, or similar things, triggering emotional outbursts.

Often people with PTSD and those with Bipolar Disorder have similar symptoms of cycling moods.

Psychiatric Medication

The term "psychiatric" refers to the medical field related to one's "psyche," psychological make-up, or mental disorders. Typically, the medication prescribed by a psychiatrist is unique to one's

---

235 Ibid., 645.

brain functioning. Types of medication include mood-stabilizing, anti-psychotic, or anti-anxiety prescriptions.

Psychotic

A description of one's thoughts when the person is not sharing the reality of the people around him. He may be hearing, seeing, or feeling things that to him are real but are not happening in the real world. His thought pattern is disorganized and may seem "crazy." His speech or behavior may appear "insane." A **psychotic break** is the event in which the person loses touch with reality and shifts into psychotic thoughts and behavior. **Psychosis** is the state one is in when he is psychotic.

Reality

Reality is an important concept in mental health; it describes what is tangible and logical and recognized by the majority of people as to what is true and real. When one is "out of touch with reality," he may be having mental health problems, particularly struggling with psychosis.

Schizophrenia Spectrum

A group of disorders that have as a prominent symptom some form of psychotic (out of touch with reality) process. The abnormalities may appear in one or more of the following areas: delusions (bizarre beliefs), hallucinations (sensory perceptions that are not based in reality but are experienced as real to the person), disorganized thinking, and abnormal physical behaviors. In addition, there are other changes evident, such as a flat and inappropriate emotional expression, and a lack of motivation for purposeful activities. Diagnoses that fall on this spectrum include **Schizophrenia** and **Schizo-Affective Disorder**. The latter disorder is a combination of the traits of schizophrenia and a mood disorder.[236]

---

236 Ibid., 87-110.

Sigmund Freud's Theory of Personality

This Austrian neurologist and father of psychoanalysis believed that mental processes were **unconscious** (i.e., not within one's awareness). He held to a threefold view of the human personality:

- The **Id**, the instinctual center of the personality, is in charge of aggressive and sexual drives.
- The **Superego** has the job of providing social and moral rules.
- The **Ego** balances the Id and the Superego in managing conflict within the psyche by using defense mechanisms and the process of **repression**.

Substance-Related and Addictive Disorders

These disorders encompass drugs of a variety of kinds (e.g., alcohol, caffeine, cannabis, opioids, tobacco, and more), which all have a common direct activation on the brain reward system when used in excess. Their use activates the pleasure system and is referred to as a "high." There are behavioral addictions such as gambling, internet gaming, sex, exercise, and shopping addictions.

Suicide

The act of taking one's own life intentionally. **Suicidal ideation** is the thought process that precedes the act. Thoughts about suicide fall on a continuum. On the benign end, a person with suicidal ideation may just wish he were dead; or he may be imagining how people would react to his death or what the world would be like if he were dead. On the potentially lethal end of the spectrum, a person may be thinking about a specific plan and organizing details in his life in order to complete the act. For this reason it is *extremely important* to take every mention of a death or suicide wish seriously, so that the lethality of the person's motives can be assessed by a professional, and any attempt stopped.

APPENDIX B
GLOSSARY OF FAITH-BASED TERMS

(Terms Used in Christian Subculture)

"As the Spirit Led Me"
This is a phrase I use to describe one of the ways to make decisions: I intentionally ask the Holy Spirit what direction or choice He wants me to make in a given situation, and then I listen for a prompting or inner voice, and follow the Spirit's lead.

Behind the Veil
After I read Blake K. Healy's book, *The Veil*,[237] I started using this term, as I wondered what was going on in my visible realm (**"this side of the veil"**) or in the spiritual world around me. Blake can see into the spiritual realm and has access to spirits (both demonic and divine) according to God's grace. I do not have that gift, but I do believe that there is spiritual dimension that some people can access. This realm, "behind the veil," reveals what is going on around us in our atmosphere in the spiritual world, not visible to the natural eye.[238]

Born-Again Christian
Reference **Encounter With the Living Christ.**

---

237 Blake K. Healy, *The Veil: An Invitation to the Unseen Realm* (Lake Mary: Charisma House, 2018).

238 Another source is H.A. Baker's *Visions Beyond the Veil: God's Revelation to Children of Heaven and Hell*. Lancaster, UK: Sovereign World, 2000.

Casting Out of a Demon

This expression is used 15 times in the New Testament specifically to refer to one aspect of Jesus's ministry. He would expel a demon or demons from a person inflicted with them by the use of His spoken word and divine authority. In the present-day church, through the power of Jesus, knowledgeable and trained Christians can identify and cast out or throw off (ekballo) a negative spiritual entity that is harming a human being. The process is often called "**deliverance.**" Some traditions refer to this as **exorcism.** All terms mean to free a person from an evil influence.

Deliverance Ministry

Reference **Casting Out of a Demon** and **Spiritual Warfare.**

"Demons at Work"

In Erin's testimony (as well as others), she experienced spiritual entities, called demons, influencing her thoughts and behaviors. A demon is a disembodied entity that has an intense craving to occupy physical bodies. A demonic spirit has a will, emotion, intelligence, self-awareness, and the ability to speak. These spirits want to shackle us with a variety of strongholds and to torment us with toxic lies, designed to kill and destroy.[239]

Devotions/Quiet Times/Meditation

While there are subtle distinctions among these three practices, each is an activity that enhances the believer's personal relationship (**soul bond**) with God. In a nutshell, each devotional involves undistracted time with God, in which reading, praying, singing, or worshipping takes place. Some refer to this experience as going into the "**secret place,**" a reference to Psalm 91:1.

Often, during my quiet time, I find Scripture that addresses a promise God gives me to solve a problem in my life. At that point, I capture those words and "**claim the Scripture.**" This is equivalent to me going to my bank (i.e., the Bible) and writing a check (i.e., God's promise) to "cover" my problem. Jesus said, "If

---

239 Prince, *They Shall Expel Demons*, 103-112.

you ask me anything in My name, I will do it."[240] I will ask for anything I want according to God's will, and the Father in heaven will give it to me. In so doing, I "claim" that Scripture.

This is one way I **"activate" the kingdom of God.** The kingdom of God is what Jesus brought to earth. The kingdom values are radically different from those of our world, and all of Jesus's ministry reveals the nature of His kingdom. When I have a time of prayer, my fundamental request is: "Thy kingdom come." I do this by paying attention to the Holy Spirit, partnering with Him, and actively seeking opportunities for evangelism, healing, or deliverance.

Encounter With the Living Christ
This describes what I believe is the **"born-again"** experience. The basic belief is that Jesus of Nazareth walked this earth as a man and was crucified as a criminal even though He was perfect and without sin. After being buried in a sealed tomb for three days, He arose from the grave, and more than 500 witnesses saw His resurrected and living body. This truth states that God's Son is the Anointed One, the Christ or the Messiah, who came to free us from sin and death, and to give us eternal life through a relationship with the Almighty God. He is the **Son of God** (John 3:16).

The act of being "born again" is often described as **receiving the Spirit of Jesus Christ into one's heart.** This is a simple act of faith. Just as though Jesus were knocking at the door of your house (heart), you open the door, and invite Him in. This is an act of surrender and renewal. When one makes this step of commitment, he becomes a **Christ-one** (a Christian).

As early as 1902, the psychologist William James wrote about **the conversion experience.** "This is a process by which a person comes to adopt an all pervasive worldview....The taking of a new

---

240 John 14:14

worldview and personal identity makes an attempt to [achieve] a curative agent for serious psychiatric maladies."[241]

Enemy of My Soul

When the word "enemy" or "enemy of my soul" is used throughout this book, the reference is to a spiritual adversary. This enemy is referred to as Satan or the devil. He is the personification of evil and is a real spiritual being who hates human beings and fosters harmful designs against mankind. For a more complete explanation, see Chapter 3. **Soul** is the person, and it is a combination of what the person thinks, feels, and chooses.

Global Awakening

This apostolic network was founded by **Randy Clark** in 1994. It is a global community of believers who are empowered to awaken the world in the areas of healing, teaching, and impartation for ministry, and to fulfill the biblical commissions of Jesus. Randy Clark was used mightily by God to begin the Toronto Blessing revival. He is the Founder and CEO of the Global Awakening School of Supernatural Ministry and the Christian Healing and Christian Prophetic Certification Programs.

"Going Down in the Spirit"

Reference **Outpourings of the Holy Spirit.**

Inner Healing

A form of healing that takes place within the soul of a person. A therapeutic/spiritual process in which wounds or traumas are touched by the Spirit-led counselor in such a way that the wounded soul achieves relief and resolution.

Outpourings of the Holy Spirit

This phrase refers to the evidence of the Holy Spirit in one's life or in the activities of a Christian community. The evidence I have seen includes physical changes in people, such as shaking,

---

241 Shafranske, *Religion and the Clinical Practice of Psychology*, 272.

For more information, refer to these biblical passages: John 3; Matthew 27 and 28; 1 Corinthians 15:6; and Revelation 3:20. Also, reference: http://www.compellingtruth.org/four-spiritual-laws.html.

swooning, or shouting. The person might describe a sense of **being anointed in the Spirit.** This experience involves miraculous healings, or being "slain" (**going down in the Spirit**), which looks like a person faints, falls asleep, or **collapses in the Spirit.** Other people have reported seeing visions, angelic beings, clouds, gold dust, and dove feathers, to name a few.

Praying in Tongues

One of the **gifts of the Spirit.** Other people may refer to this gift as *glossolalia.* It is an action used by a Christian in which he speaks in an unknown language. This was first mentioned in Acts 2:4 (New Living Translation), upon the day of **Pentecost,** "And everyone present was filled with the Holy Spirit and began speaking in other languages, as the Holy Spirit gave them this ability." From my point of view, the experience is like singing or reciting poetry but in a language even I, the speaker, cannot understand. The practice edifies me and helps me to pray in alignment with God's will. I also refer to it as **praying in the Holy Spirit.**

Other gifts of the Spirit include teaching, healing, miracles, and prophesying, to name a few. See 1 Corinthians 12-14. One of the gifts is a **word of knowledge.** This is when an idea or image comes to a person (i.e., he "receives" a word of knowledge) that the Holy Spirit is transmitting, which is knowledge that only God knows, and one could not know by human means. It is listed as one of the spiritual gifts in 1 Corinthians 12:8.

Pre-Fall State

This description is my term for describing the human being the way our Creator saw him before the person "sinned." Specifically, I try to relate to any person as he would have appeared in God's paradise garden. That means assessing him as perfect from the start before the enemy caused him to rebel against God. With these lenses, I am not denying or ignoring the person's current faults and weaknesses, but, rather, I am covering them with the lens of Jesus in my mind's eye. I am seeing him as "righteous" or "all right," flawless, as he was intended to be originally, just as Father God sees him if he confesses that Christ is his Savior and Lord. This way of looking at people frees me from being critical and judgmental.

Rational Worldview
A rational worldview holds to the belief that the supreme authority in matters of opinion and knowledge is reason alone, and all knowledge is based on tangible evidence. In theology, **rationalism** is the doctrine that human reason, unaided by divine revelation, is the sole guide to obtaining truth. This worldview is similar to **humanism,** which believes that human reason and scientific inquiry should replace belief in God. Rationalism contrasts with the supernatural perspective, while humanism is juxtaposed to one that believes in a God-centered philosophy.

Secret Place
Reference **Devotions/Quiet Times/Meditation**.

Sharing the Lord
This is an evangelical practice during which a person opens up about her faith in Jesus, and shares basic ideas of how and why Jesus died for a person's sins. The purpose in "sharing the Lord" is to encourage the listener to receive Jesus as Savior and Lord.

Signs of Revival
A revival is a spiritual phenomenon in which people experience God in a variety of ways. Some are brought under conviction in their conscience and repent, and surrender to Jesus. This is the experience of **salvation.** Some witness an encounter with the Holy Spirit in which a divine prophetic word or infusing of a "calling" occurs. These are **impartations.** Many receive **healing** either miraculously (i.e., completely and immediately) or in increments progressing toward full healing. Sometimes, the person is **delivered** and feels a negative energy or demonic spirit leave him. During a revival, a believer might **pray over** another person by laying a hand on the receiver's shoulder, head, or back, or even the injured body part, in order to bring God's healing in the name of Jesus.

Soul Bond
Reference **Devotions/Quiet Times/Meditation**.

Spiritual Warfare
There are terms used throughout this book that fall under the category of spiritual warfare. (Refer to the sections on "Practical Steps to Handling Suffering" and "The Doctrine of Deliverance in a Nutshell.") In brief, I believe there is an **enemy, Satan,** who intends to destroy our lives in various ways. The devil's team consists of **demonic entities, called demons.** According to Derek Prince, a **demon** is a disembodied spirit that has marks of personality, with a will, emotions, intellect, self-awareness, and the ability to speak.[242]

Because of spiritual warfare, we have been given Jesus's blood as a weapon of destruction. Jesus, the Messiah, was crucified, and **shed His blood** on the cross for the purpose of defeating our spiritual enemy. When we activate the name of Jesus, the devil and his team must leave. When the enemy attacks any one of us, Christians are given **authority through Jesus** to rebuke (i.e., terminate the influence of) and cast off the enemy or his minions. Sometimes, the demonic entity is a **stronghold** or thought system, which also can be eradicated by Jesus.

When a person is set free from the demonic influence, it is necessary to fill his or her spiritual void (left by the fleeing spiritual entity) with an aspect of God's divine power. This is called the *divine exchange.* Specifically, Jesus carried away the "bad," and the Holy Spirit exchanged it for the "good." For example, if one renounces fear, he needs to call in love. If he has cast off lying, he fills himself with God's truth. If he rebukes physical or emotional pain, he claims healing. This process describes **deliverance.**

"The Holy Spirit Entered Me."
This phrase describes my witnessing a change in my inner being because the Holy Spirit has come into my spirit and changed my soul. For me, it was (and continues to be) as concrete as my stepping into a steam bath, or walking through a swirl of wind, or

---

242 Prince, *They Shall Expel Demons,* 103.

entering a dark room and then turning the lights on. There is an experiential change in my thoughts, emotions, and decision-making, all for the good. I feel **connected with God.** It is the same as being **born again.** This commitment to Jesus is an act of surrendering one's reliance on the physical life and giving up the need for "the flesh" (i.e., that which is seen). This process is often called **dying to self.**

When one surrenders to the Spirit of God, he has invited Jesus into his heart *and* has developed a hunger and thirst for Him. I often describe a person as **"drinking in the Holy Spirit"** because when this happens, he develops an unquenchable thirst for God's Spirit. He is eager to seek Him, ask about Him, and enjoy His presence. When the Holy Spirit connects with a passage of Scripture in a powerful way as to touch one's heart, we call the encounter a **rhema** word.

Theophostic Prayer Ministry (TPM)
Founded by Ed M. Smith, a Baptist minister, in 1996. TPM is an approach to "mind renewal," or the healing of emotional pain. **Sozo** is a similar approach to inner healing, incorporating body-soul-spirit. Sozo is not a counseling session but a time of interacting with Father, Son, and Holy Spirit for wholeness. Both TPM and sozo focus on the three components of Jesus's ministry: salvation, healing, and deliverance.[243]

The Persecuted Church
Voice of the Martyrs and other international organizations help raise awareness and funds for Christians around the world who are being tortured, arrested, ridiculed, and otherwise tormented because they publicly claim to believe in Jesus Christ. Christians who reside in these eastern hemisphere countries (usually) are part of a worldwide **Persecuted Church.**[244]

---

243 For more information, reference: en.wikipedia.org/wiki/Theophostic_counseling,

http://www.womenofgrace.com/blog/?p=73, and http://www.bethelsozo.com.

244 For more information, reference: https://billygraham.org/story/franklin-graham-sheds-light-

christian-persecution-new-tv-special and https://vom.com.au/persecution/.

Walk by Faith
A phrase that describes the spiritual manner in which one goes about his daily life, i.e., "he walks through life." But the phrase "by faith" means he has a different mindset, one that is distinct from "walking by sight." Most people who don't believe in God use a "sight" approach, which is a rational, tangible, and scientific way to determine what is going on around them. What is real is what they see, feel, touch, and taste, and what they can prove by hard evidence. A Christ-one desires to approach life based on faith, which are promises in the Bible and happenings connected to the heavenly realms and going on **behind the veil**. What is based on faith cannot be seen, touched, or tasted, nor is there objective evidence for most of it. (There are exceptions to this rule. I saw concrete evidence of God's activity when my broken, twisted wrist bone experienced a warming sensation and visibly straightened at the time God healed it on October 22, 2015, around 9:00 p.m.)

Word of Knowledge
Reference **Praying in Tongues**.

BOOK REFERENCES

Allender, D. B. (1999). *The Healing Path: How the Hurts in Your Past Can Lead You to a More Abundant Life*. New York: Random House.

Baker, H. A. (2000). *Visions Beyond the Veil: God's Revelation to Children of Heaven and Hell*. Lancaster, UK: Sovereign World.

Baker, M. W. (2007). *Jesus, The Greatest Therapist Who Ever Lived*. New York: HarperOne.

Bosworth, F. F. (2000). *Christ the Healer: Sermons on Divine Healing*. Grand Rapids: Baker Books.

Botkin, B. A. (1945). *Lay My Burden Down: A Folk History of Slavery*. Chicago, IL: Phoenix.

Brown, C. G. (2013). *The Healing Gods: Complementary and Alternative Medicine in Christian America*. New York: Oxford University Press.

Caton, J. (2014). *Heart of Deception: Cara Moore's True Story of an On-Line Dating Scam*. Batavia, NY: Hi-Tek.

Caton, J. (2011). *White Heart: A Novel*. Mustang, OK: Tate Publishing.

Clark, R. (2009). *The Thrill of Victory/The Agony of Defeat*. Mechanicsburg: Apostolic Network of Global Awakening.

Cramer, R. L. (1959). *Psychology of Jesus and Mental Health*. Grand Rapids, MI: Zondervan.

Crandall, C. W. (2010). *Raising the Dead: A Doctor Encounters the Miraculous*. New York: FaithWords.

Crandall, C. W., & Bearss, K. (2016). *Touching Heaven: A Cardiologist's Encounters With Death and Living Proof of an Afterlife*. New York: FaithWords.

Dekker, T. (2018). *The 49th Mystic: Beyond the Circle*. Grand Rapids, MI: Revell.

Diagnostic and Statistical Manual of Mental Disorders (5th ed.). (2013). Arlington, VA: American Psychiatric Publishing.

Erikson, E. H. (1950). *Childhood and Society*. New York: W.W. Norton and Co.

Erikson, E. H. (1962). *Young Man Luther: A Study in Psychoanalysis and History*. New York: W.W. Norton & Co.

Erikson, E. H., & Schlein, S. (1987). *A Way of Looking at Things: Selected Papers From 1930-1980*. New York: Norton.

Fraiberg, S. (1959). *The Magic Years: Understanding and Handling the Problems of Early Childhood*. New York: Scribner.

Frankl, V. E. (1955). *The Doctor and the Soul; An Introduction to Logotherapy. Tr. From the German*. New York: Knopf.

Friedman, L. J. (1999). *Identity's Architect: A Biography of Erik H. Erikson*. New York: Scribner.

Healy, B. K. (2018). *The Veil: An Invitation to the Unseen Realm*. Lake Mary, FL: Charisma House.

Hetland, L. (2017). *Called to Reign: Living and Loving From a Place of Rest*. New York: Convergence PR LLC.

Hogue, R. (2008). *Forgiveness*. Instantpublisher.com.

Horrobin, P. (2008). *Healing Through Deliverance: Foundation and Practice of Deliverance Ministry*. Grand Rapids, MI: Chosen Books.

Hyder, O. Q. (1971). *The Christian's Handbook of Psychiatry.* Old Tappan, NJ: Fleming H. Revell Company.

Ilibagiza, I. (2006). *Left to Tell: Discovering God Amidst the Rwandan Holocaust.* Carlsbad: Hay House.

Johnson, B. (2009). *The Happy Intercessor.* Shippensburg: Destiny Image Pubishers.

Jordan, M. J. (2014). *Sonship: A Journey into Father's Heart.* Taupo, New Zealand: Fatherheart Media.

Koenig, H. G. (2005). *Faith and Mental Health: Religious Resources for Healing.* Philadelphia, PA: Templeton Foundation Press.

Mangis, M. W. (2008). *Signature Sins: Taming Our Wayward Hearts.* Downers Grove: IVP Books.

Newberg, A. B., DAquili, E. G., & Rause, V. (2001). *Why God Won't Go Away: Brain Science and the Biology of Belief.* New York: Ballantine Books.

Nouwen, H. J. (1972). *The Wounded Healer.* Garden City: Doubleday.

Pargament, K. I. (2007). *Spiritually Integrated Psychotherapy: Understanding and Addressing the Sacred.* New York: Guilford.

Pert, C. B. (1997). *Molecules of Emotion: Why You Feel the Way You Feel.* New York: Scribner.

Prince, D. (1998). *They Shall Expel Demons.* Grand Rapids: Chosen Books.

Rogers, C. R. (1961). *On Becoming a Person: A Therapist's View of Psychotherapy.* Boston, MA: Houghton Mifflin.

Shafranske, E. P. (1996). *Religion and the Clinical Practice of Psychology.* Washington, DC: American Psychological Association.

Sorge, B. (2015). *Pain, Perplexity and Promotion: A Prophetic Interpretation of the Book of Job*. Lees Summit, MO: Oasis House.

Sorge, B. (2001). *Secrets of the Secret Place: Keys to Igniting Your Personal Time With God*. Kansas City: Oasis House.

Sweet, L. I., & Viola, F. (2012). *Jesus: A Theography*. Nashville: Thomas Nelson.

Tada, J. E. (2012). *Making Sense of Suffering*. Peabody: Aspire Press.

Vine, W. E. (1997). *Vines Expository Dictionary of Old & New Testament Words*. Nashville, TN: T. Nelson Publishers.

Virkler, M., & Virkler, P. (2010). *4 keys to hearing Gods voice*. Shippensburg, PA: Destiny Image.

Whittemore, A. G. (1964). *Joy in Holiness: A Collection of Letters and Other Writings of Spiritual Direction*. West Park, NY: Holy Cross Publications.

Zadai, K. L., & Roth, S. (2019). *The Agenda of Angels: What the Holy Ones Want You to Know About the Next Move of God*. Shippensburg, PA: DestinyImage.

If you appreciated *Soul Pain Revealed:*
Bridging Psychology With Faith as the Way Through Suffering,
kindly consider leaving a review at *Amazon* or *Goodreads.*

Dr. Julie Caton would love to connect with you
in the following ways:

www.drjuliecaton.com

facebook.com/DrJulieCaton/

drjuliecaton@gmail.com

81 North Main Street, Oakfield, New York 14125
585-993-5111

Updates on future publications can be found at:

 **GROUND TRUTH PRESS**
P.O. Box 7313
Nashua, NH 03060-7313

www.groundtruthpress.com